'Fiona is a fabulous phenomenon who literally changes lives and to whom I am eternally grateful' *Diana Foster-Smith, mother and show jumper*

'Coaching with Fiona provided me with a framework within which to change the way that I viewed life. In each session, she imbued me with a huge amount of energy as well as concrete goals to achieve this change' *Jamie Kerr, property developer*

'When I met Fiona, I knew I wanted to do something but just didn't know what. She helped me focus, take action and enabled me to move forward. Fiona is the light at the end of the tunnel' *Debra Lennie, The Debra Lennie Home Care Service*

'Don't enter into the experience lightly – Fiona expects commitment and results as much as you do. A woman who has had a fascinating life and with that knowledge and experience will bring some enlightenment to your world' *David Hindmarch, MD, Chandlers Oil & Gas Ltd*

'When I made the decision to truly live up to my potential I was terrified – not of failure, but of what successes I could achieve. Part of me felt ashamed for thinking I could be so much. Since I began working with Fiona not only have I owned up to my dreams, I have claimed them, embraced them and commenced working passionately towards achieving them. This is nothing short of life changing.' *Domonique Bertolucci, Management Consultant*

'Fiona's challenging, perceptive and just a little scarcy . . . in 4 weeks I've increased my earnings, expanded my client base and finally got the exercise habit. I've always known how to set goals but working with Fiona I've developed the motivation and courage to take action and achieve them. Fiona is outstanding, she really delivers. Somehow she broke through all my excuses, helped overcome my fears and together we developed ideas and techniques which have enabled me to unlock my potential for success and happiness. I've learnt how to overcome setbacks, step out of my comfort zone and make life-changing decisions' *Sheena Doneghan, Director, Enterprise Alliance.*

Be Your *Own* Life Coach

HOW TO TAKE CONTROL OF YOUR LIFE AND
ACHIEVE YOUR WILDEST DREAMS

Fiona Harrold

Hodder & Stoughton

Copyright © 2000 by Fiona Harrold

First published in Great Britain in 2000 by Hodder and Stoughton
A division of Hodder Headline

The right of Fiona Harrold to be identified as the Author of the
Work has been asserted by her in accordance with the
Copyright, Designs and Patents Act 1988.

10 9 8 7 6 5 4 3

A CIP catalogue record for this title is available from the British Library.

ISBN 0 340 77028 7

Typeset by Hewer Text Ltd, Edinburgh
Printed and bound in Great Britain by
Mackays of Chatham PLC, Chatham, Kent

Hodder and Stoughton
A division of Hodder Headline
338 Euston Road
London NW1 3BH

To my darling Dad, Michael Harrold.
The Best.

Our deepest fear is not that we are inadequate
Our deepest fear is that we are powerful beyond measure
It is our light, not our darkness, that most frightens us.
We ask ourselves:
'Who am I to be brilliant, gorgeous, talented, fabulous?'
Actually, who are you not to be?
You are a child of God.
Your playing small doesn't serve the world.
There is nothing enlightening about shrinking so that other people
around you won't feel insecure.
We are all meant to shine as children do.
We are born to manifest the glory of God that is within us.
It is not just in some of us; it is in everyone.
And as we let our light shine, we unconsciously give other people
permission to do the same.
As we are liberated from our own fear, our presence automatically
releases others.

Marianne Williamson

ACKNOWLEDGEMENTS

A heartfelt thank-you to Caro Handley for her constant support in getting this book out of me! Thanks to Rowena Webb at Hodder & Stoughton for keeping faith in me. Thanks to my agent, Judith Chilcote, for just the right amount of cajoling. Thanks for everything to my great friend and rock, Don Ford. Finally, huge thanks and admiration to all my clients past and present, who all live fearless lives.

CONTENTS

CHAPTER ONE

BE THE BEST: SIGN HERE AND CREATE THE LIFE YOU'VE ALWAYS WANTED

M Y EARLIEST memory of a life-changing realisation took place when I was no more than eleven or twelve. The circumstances that prompted it have long since faded, but the sharpness and impact of the moment are with me now. It was a realisation that was to shape my life forever more. What I understood was simply this: that the greatest tragedy of a lifetime must be to live with regret – to reach a point where you were confronted with all the things you had not done, or even tried. I made a decision there and then to do and to try all the things I ever dreamed of, so that I would live my life – and look back at the end of it – without regret.

Since then my life has been shaped by that early decision. For example, this book *had* to be written. I knew that if I shirked the challenge I would – without a shadow of doubt – be accruing a major regret for some later day or year.

I feel incredibly lucky to have been prompted to think in this way at such an early age. And the credit for that belongs to my dad, who was a self-improvement fanatic long before anyone else around us had heard of the concept. My father grew up on a farm in southern Ireland, left school at fourteen and headed over to England to join his older brother to look for a life of possibilities beyond the quiet rural life he had known. After the war he settled in Northern Ireland, married my mother and got a job as a door-to-door salesman with the Hoover Company. He spent his working day knocking on doors, selling vacuum cleaners and washing machines. Within two months he was selling more than anyone else in the entire country, including men who had been doing the job for years. My father was in his element and he became fascinated by the psychology of selling and of human potential and success. He began reading everything he could find about these subjects and attended Dale Carnegie seminars. Dale was trained by Norman Vincent Peale, the founding father of American 'can-do' philosophy whose book *The Power of Positive Thinking* has sold over thirty-four million copies. He believed that anyone can be anything, regardless of circumstance. From the age of eleven onwards, I was introduced to early self-improvement pioneers such as Napoleon Hill, Clement Stone and titles like *Stop Worrying and Start Living, How to Win Friends and Influence People*, and *Grow Rich While You Sleep!* Dad would come home from seminars in Belfast fired up with the latest revelations he had absorbed, evangelical in his determination to pass on the golden nuggets – the secrets of success. Being the best, extracting the best from himself, became his mission and I was keen to learn alongside. His gift to me was quite simply to take me seriously and to believe in my ability to do anything I wanted to do – and I mean anything. He saw me and taught me to see myself as someone with very special even phenomenal talents and potential.

From a young age I learned that life is wide open and that

everything and anything is possible. Dad taught me that the only real limitations in life come from inside – not outside – us. My father never dampened my enthusiasm or scoffed at me; he took all my ambitions seriously and always supported me. When I decided I wanted to be a newsreader at the age of thirteen, my father suggested that it would be a good idea to soften my strong Irish accent. From that moment on I adopted what's known in Belfast as a 'Malone Road' accent. I went to school the next day speaking as though I'd spent my life on Belfast's smartest road! The crucial point here is that my father believed, and therefore I did too, that whatever I wanted was attainable. He believed in me and he taught me to believe in myself. He was, in fact, my first Life Coach. It was, of course, a few more years before I made the decision to become a Life Coach myself. And in the intervening time I went through a crisis that taxed my self-belief to its limits.

My father died when I was twenty, a loss that affected me very deeply. I moved to England and became involved in radical politics. I moved into a squat – a near-derelict house in South London – that I shared with other like-minded radicals. They saw themselves as victims of the government, the council and any other authority that happened to be around. They drank too much, smoked too much and spent their time plotting to change the world.

For me the end result of getting involved in this attitude to life was total exhaustion, illness and depression. I spent eighteen months suffering from chronic fatigue and struggling to get my life back on course. Eventually I moved out of the squat and away from the people with whom I'd been involved. Unimpressed by a doctor who offered me pills to help me sleep and pills to wake me up I began to explore other ways of getting my life back on track.

I tried virtually every alternative therapy, from homeopathy to iridology through Chinese herbs to reflexology and acupuncture. Many of them were helpful. Then I met a woman who was to take up where my father left off. She gave 'intuitive massage' that is, massage based on her intuitive healing abilities, and called herself a self-esteem consultant, something I had never heard of before. She worked with me to rediscover my childhood optimism and enthusiasm.

By the time I had fully recovered, I had apprenticed myself to her and I spent the next eighteen months learning everything she could teach me. When she retired I took over her practice and although I've been through a couple of other careers on the way to Life Coaching, I have never looked back since that time.

What my illness taught me was that your mindset shapes everything else in your life. When I joined people who felt powerless and angry I began to feel that way, too. And I chose an environment that supported those beliefs. My energy levels, my health and my feelings about life were all deeply affected. It forced me to re-evaluate my life and I made the decision to reinforce my self-belief, just as my father had, and to be with people who would support me. I began, once again, to feel light-hearted, positive and confident. I understood that the mental outlook, the beliefs and the thoughts I chose would shape the rest of my life.

MY COMMITMENT TO YOU

We are embarking on an adventure together and my intention is to do for you what my father did for me. I will think of you, speak to you and work alongside you with absolute faith in you and your abilities. I will have high expectations for you and I will want the very best for you. I will believe in your phenomenal potential to do, have and be whatever you want.

I will look at you in terms of the vast potential you have, and I will show you how the one obstacle that holds you back is the way you see yourself. My job will be to help you to move beyond those doubts and fears that hold you back. Whatever the limiting beliefs you have, it is never too late to change them, and to create a high level of self-belief. And when you believe in yourself – totally and with conviction – then you will be able to do and achieve anything you want.

However you see your life and whatever is your ideal, you can be sure that it will involve doing something that fulfils, excites and enthrals you. And in this book I am going to help you to achieve that something. This adventure will take courage, determination and commitment from you, and in return I will give you 100 percent commitment. My promise to you is that if you choose to work with me, through the steps laid out in this book, then your life will change in ways that will take your breath away. You will be challenged and I will demand motivation and effort from you. There may be times when you feel like giving up or throwing this book across the room, but if you stick with it, you will feel a sense of achievement that can only be described as pure joy. You will have the thrill of liking yourself in a way that you never thought possible. You will feel the profound satisfaction that comes from reaching beyond what is easy and comfortable, towards the dreams and goals that bring true, deep fulfilment.

My greatest joy will be to support you in believing in yourself, so that you can unlock the door to your creativity and enormous potential. I will be the midwife to your genius! I will be there for you every step of the way, coaxing and cajoling, keeping you strong when you falter and celebrating your victories.

Over the years I have gone through this process with many clients and it has been and continues to be enormously rewarding. I have watched people move from uncertainty and self-doubt into certainty and self-belief, and to blossom in ways they hadn't thought possible.

Caroline's story

Caroline is a wonderful example of what I'm talking about. I worked with her for a television programme. She had written in saying she'd love to get back to work now that her children were settled at school, but that she didn't have any idea what she could do.

Caroline was an immensely likeable, bubbly 38-year-old who oozed warmth and personality. In our first session I asked her about all the things she enjoyed doing, both now and in her pre-children days. It turned out that she adored transforming rooms, flats and entire houses from dull, uninviting spaces into warm, homely cocoons. Needless to say I soon discovered that she was absolutely brilliant at doing this and could do it on a shoestring budget. We came up with a totally new business concept, which we called 'The Caroline Kerr Home Service – Turning Your House into a Home'. It was aimed at time-poor, busy professionals who simply didn't have time to create the kind of homes they would like to live in.

Caroline could see what a great idea this was, but felt uncomfortable about asking for money for something that had been her hobby. The thought of being paid for doing something she enjoyed brought out all her doubts and uncertainties. Over the next few weeks I concentrated on increasing her sense of self-worth and focused on the immense value she had to offer to potential customers. She learned to replace her old, limiting beliefs with new ones, such as: 'I am good enough' and 'other people enjoy

PAYING ME FOR MY WORK'. SHE SOON BEGAN TO BELIEVE IN HERSELF.

AS SHE WAS INVENTING AN ENTIRELY NEW SERVICE WITHOUT ANY PRECEDENT, THERE WAS NO SCALE OF FEES FOR HER TO USE. IT WAS UP TO HER TO CREATE ONE. I SUGGESTED THAT SHE BE PLAYFUL AND FLEXIBLE WITH HER PRICING AND TO CHARGE A FEE WITH WHICH SHE FELT COMFORTABLE, KNOWING THAT SHE COULD CHANGE IT WITH THE NEXT CLIENT.

OVER THE WEEKS THE PROGRAMME'S VIEWERS FOLLOWED CAROLINE'S PROGRESS AND SAW HER CONFIDENCE LEVELS SOAR AS SHE CAME TO BELIEVE IN HERSELF AND TO SEE HERSELF AS THE VERY TALENTED YOUNG WOMAN SHE WAS. WHEN I FIRST MET HER SHE WAS MODEST TO THE POINT OF DISMISSING HER TALENTS, INSISTING THAT ANYONE COULD DO WHAT SHE DID. BUT BY THE END OF THE FIRST MONTH SHE WAS IN ABSOLUTELY NO DOUBT ABOUT HER UNIQUE TALENTS AND POTENTIAL, AND SHE WAS BEGINNING TO SEE ALL THE OPPORTUNITIES AND POSSIBILITIES THAT WERE AVAILABLE TO HER.

CAROLINE'S NEXT STEP WAS TO APPROACH A MAJOR SCOTTISH NEWSPAPER. THEY INTERVIEWED HER AND PRINTED A FEATURE ABOUT HER BUSINESS. THE RESULT? CAROLINE ACQUIRED HER FIRST PAYING CLIENT — A PROFESSIONAL WOMAN WHO HAD JUST MOVED INTO A NEW FLAT AND NEEDED THE ENTIRE PLACE REDECORATED. SHE WAS OVERJOYED TO FIND CAROLINE AND AFTER THEIR FIRST MEETING HIRED HER TO DO UP THE WHOLE FLAT. THE CAROLINE KERR HOME SERVICE WAS UP AND RUNNING.

Like Caroline, you deserve to be doing something that uses your particular talents and abilities – something that you really enjoy. You deserve to be living a life that excites and fulfils you.

WHAT I WILL DO FOR YOU

As your Life Coach, I will work with you to create your ideal life. So let me explain just how we'll do this. Life Coaching as I practise it involves three aspects, all of which are equally important:

- First, I will believe in you totally and I will demonstrate my belief by taking you and your desires seriously.
- Second, I will encourage you to show faith in yourself and to believe in yourself. I will consistently feed your self-belief so that it will grow and flourish, and with it your confidence will too.
- Third, I will define, with you, a plan of action for achieving your goals and desires and I will keep you on track towards them.

When I take on a new client I ask them to sign a contract agreeing the terms under which I will Coach them. I then ask them to write down a little background information about themselves, some of their goals, their expectations and the things they like about themselves. I also ask them to look at the things they might like to change.

Next, I talk to them face to face or by telephone for an hour, during which I encourage them to get really clear about what they want and then we draw up a plan of action. After this we speak at appointed times every week. These times are agreed in advance and I insist that we stick to them. Without real commitment, Coaching won't work. At the end of each session I give each client specific assignments and challenges that I ask them to complete before the next session. Again, I expect these to be completed.

At this stage it's important to clarify the difference between therapy or counselling and Coaching, as I practise it.

Therapy can be enormously beneficial for some people, but it usually involves looking backwards and creating a picture of yourself as someone with issues that handicap you in life. This works in the opposite way to what I'm doing through Coaching. I'm not interested in looking backwards and focusing on what hasn't worked or on things that have been painful.

Some of my most difficult clients have been those who've spent years in therapy. Everything that happens in the present gets linked to something in the past and this often becomes a handicap to moving forward because they don't believe that change can be easy and uncomplicated. They have plenty of excuses for not taking action – plenty of explanations and justifications. But this kind of attitude is very different from mine.

Coaching moves people forward, fast and easily. Some people have called it 'Bootcamp Coaching', and I admit that I'm demanding and I can be tough. I'm not going to be soft on you. I want action, not excuses. I never mollycoddle my clients or see them as people with problems and issues. I see them as healthy, strong and capable. My expectations are high, because I know that when I expect the best of someone, they give their best.

And this is the way I will be Coaching you. I will ask you to sign a contract with me at the end of this chapter. I'll ask you to work with this book every week, for a time that is put aside for this purpose. I will give you exercises and set you challenges and assignments that I will expect you to meet. And together we will examine every single area of your life and look at what's working and what isn't so that we can clear the way for what you truly want.

MY PROMISE TO YOU
If you are willing to do your part and to stick with me, then I will promise you the following in return:

- I will instil in you indestructible self-belief and teach you how to eliminate the doubts and limitations that hold you back.
- I will train you to be mentally fit and agile, to think like a natural optimist, to expect to succeed and to handle setbacks quickly and easily.
- I will help you to clarify your desires, dreams and ambitions into precise goals.
- I will motivate you to take action.

As we work together you will achieve the mental strength and flexibility of a world-class athlete, performing at your peak, competing against yourself to surpass your personal bests and enjoying yourself immensely as you do so. You will find that the stronger and more determined you grow, the harder you'll be able to push yourself, so that you will be amazed by the extent of your abilities.

You will join the very small percentage of people who truly fulfil their potential. You will join the ranks of my clients and seminar participants who live their lives fearlessly and passionately.

YOUR COMMITMENT TO YOURSELF

I want you to use me as your Coach and this book as your guide to achieve your own personal mission – the quest to fulfil your true potential and to begin to live your ideal life. My clients get results; some of them get extraordinary results. I give each one my undivided attention. I expect, want and demand the very best from them and I want the very best for them. I bring 100 percent of myself to each client; I am totally committed to them and their goals. So why is it that one client will do well while another will do brilliantly? Why will one achieve good results while another gets stunning results? What makes that vital difference? Is it luck, circumstances, star signs? Absolutely not.

Over my years of working with hundreds of clients I have seen, time after time, what makes the vital difference and I can tell you what it is with absolute certainty. It is the degree of commitment to themselves and their goals that each client has when I work with them. So it's important, at this stage, that you understand what this commitment is about and you must be willing to give it. Only when you do so can you achieve fantastic results in your life.

This commitment is made up of four distinct elements:

- motivation
- self-belief
- self-discipline
- willingness to challenge

Let's look at these four aspects in a little more detail:

Motivation
This is the measure of how much you want to bring change into your life and it is the most important factor of all. Are you truly ready for change? Are you sick enough of how things have been? Have you had enough of struggle, worry, loneliness, insecurity, feeling second best and thinking 'if only'? If you have and you're willing to do something big about it then your motivation will be high.

Self-belief
This is the degree to which you believe, deep inside, that you are worthy and deserving of the good things that you are about to bring into your life. Without it you will sabotage and resist these good things. Your self-belief may not be perfect, but what's really important at this stage is that you are willing – with my help – to increase your self-belief.

11

Self-discipline

This is a vital quality, because when the going gets tough it will be your self-discipline that keeps you moving forward. It's easy to be enthusiastic, and to work hard and go for it when things are going well. But change always involves a certain amount of discomfort and there will be days when you don't feel like trying, or when you have a setback. At these times it's important that you keep going, and self-discipline will be your ally.

Willingness to challenge

This is about being willing to challenge yourself and everything you know, including things that you have believed about yourself and the world all your life. This challenge is necessary to create new ways of thinking and being, and to allow a vast new range of possibilities into your life. If you stick with the known and the familiar you'll rule out the new and end up staying just where you are.

All the help, support and inspiration I can provide for you has to be ignited by your commitment. You must be prepared to stoke the fires of your own self-belief and to handle the inevitable difficulties and setbacks quickly and usefully. You must be willing to suspend your disbelief and believe that the things you want are possible.

This will require you to be the best that you can possibly be and to take responsibility for creating the life you want. And, most importantly, you will need to develop a healthy working relationship with yourself.

If, at any time, you feel the momentum has slowed and you feel sluggish or uncertain then come back to this section. You will have lapsed in one or more of the four elements of commitment and will need to refresh and renew those aspects.

Nicole's story

NICOLE WAS A SUCCESSFUL NATIONAL NEWSPAPER JOURNALIST WITH WHAT MANY PEOPLE CONSIDERED TO BE AN ENVIABLE LIFE. SHE CAME TO ME BECAUSE SHE WASN'T DOING THE ONE THING THAT SHE HAD WANTED TO DO SINCE SHE WAS SEVEN: WRITING NOVELS. AT THIRTY-SEVEN, THE DEMANDS OF HER CAREER MEANT THAT HER DREAM HAD BEEN SHELVED.

NICOLE'S BELIEF IN HER ABILITY TO WRITE A NOVEL HAD REACHED AN ALL-TIME LOW, BUT SHE FELT SHE HAD TO TRY OR SHE WOULD ALWAYS BE LEFT WONDERING 'WHAT IF'?

I ASKED HER TO COME UP WITH AN IDEA FOR HER BOOK AND TO WRITE A CHAPTER JUST FOR ME, SUSPENDING ANY CRITICISM OR JUDGEMENT ABOUT IT. THE CHAPTER ARRIVED ALONG WITH AN OUTLINE OF THE REST OF THE BOOK. I LOVED IT AND FOUND MYSELF LAUGHING OUT LOUD WHILE READING IT ON A TRAIN JOURNEY. NICOLE WROTE ANOTHER THREE CHAPTERS AND SENT IT OFF TO A LEADING LITERARY AGENT WHO CALLED HER IMMEDIATELY; HE WANTED TO TAKE HER ON AS A CLIENT. SHE'S NOW SIGNED WITH HIS AGENCY AND IS FINISHING HER NOVEL.

THE IMPORTANT THING ABOUT NICOLE'S STORY IS THAT SHE WANTED TO MOVE FORWARD SO MUCH THAT SHE WAS WILLING TO DO THE WORK — PUT PEN TO PAPER AND THEN TAKE THE RISK OF LETTING SOMEONE ELSE SEE IT. NICOLE SHOWED TOTAL COMMITMENT AND WILLINGNESS TO TAKE THE RISKS AND THE ACTIONS NECESSARY. AS A RESULT, HER CONFIDENCE LEVELS HAVE RISEN DRAMATICALLY AND SHE CAN NOW SEE A WHOLE NEW WAY OF LIFE OPENING UP FOR HER.

YOUR IDEAL LIFE

Before we go on to look at how you will create your ideal life you have to know what it is. Perhaps you imagine that this is the easiest part. Would you be a millionaire, able to give up work and have fun for the rest of your life? Do you picture yourself lying on a beach somewhere hot and beautiful, the crystal blue waves lapping at your feet?

Well, let's face it: who doesn't have fantasies like these sometimes? But that's the point: these are fantasies. To find your *true* ideal life you have to look a little further. What would you do after a month lying on the beach, when you got bored and restless? The reason why this book is not simply a manual on how to become a millionaire – though, of course, you might become one – is because what we actually want is far more than just money.

I used to have a very set picture of what an ideal life would be like, and I imagined that we all shared the same picture. I thought that everyone probably wanted roughly the same things in their working life – plenty of money, short working hours and a high-achieving job. It was a London cab driver who taught me to look at things very differently.

He was driving me home one night and chatting away, as cabbies do. He told me that he had two jobs: he worked during the day as a welder, then showered and changed and spent the evening in his cab. I started to sympathise with him about his long working hours and how tough it must be.

'Poor you,' I said.

He looked surprised. 'Why do you say that?' he asked. 'I'm really happy with what I do. I have a good laugh with the lads during the day and then I have a great time in the cab at night. When I drop you off now I'll wait until you've got safely inside your front door and I'll know I've done a good job.'

What he said turned my ideas about an ideal life inside out. I realised that he was living his ideal life and it was uniquely his. What makes up the picture of an ideal life is totally individual for each of us. Since then I have been endlessly fascinated and moved by the ideal lives that my clients have dreamed up for themselves. And I have had the deep satisfaction of working with each of them to make those dreams come true. I have discovered, without exception, that the dream each person has is totally in keeping with who they are and, as a result, totally achievable.

Think about what it is that really satisfies you – what gives you a sense of achievement. What absorbs you so much that you don't notice time passing. What is it that excites you, that you love doing so much you'd feel truly lucky to be able to do it all the time.

Most of us know, deep down, what we really want to be doing. But we normally keep it very private, because we think it's impossible to actually make a living doing something we enjoy so much. Perhaps it's a hobby at the moment; perhaps it's only a dream, but it's certainly there, somewhere.

Then think about the rest of your life: your relationships, your home and your lifestyle. What would you like to change, add or improve?

Exercise

Now I want you to spend a few minutes writing down five things you've always wanted to do but haven't got around to so far, or have dismissed as impossible. Don't think about this for too long. Just start writing and see what you come up with.

Write down, beside each goal, two reasons why you haven't managed it so far. This will give you a starting point for your Coaching work, because these reasons will give you a clear indication of how you see yourself and what your limiting beliefs are.

Make a list of five ways in which your life would be different if you used this book to transform the way you see yourself. How would someone know from looking at your life that you were fearlessly living out your potential, taking risks, handling setbacks and living the life you truly want?

Keep what you have written, because towards the end of the book you can look back and see what progress you've made.

Did you want a change of career? A career shift upwards? A new or improved relationship? More money? Better health? More time for yourself? Did you see yourself working harder, or working less, using your time more constructively, being appreciated for your wonderful work, in a loving, satisfying relationship?

Whether your goals feel absolutely impossible, or whether you've already taken some tentative steps along the path towards one or more of them, now is the time to make them a reality.

Work with me, through the rest of this book and I will give you the confidence, the self-belief, the courage and the determination to achieve whatever it is that you want most in the world.

OUR CONTRACT

Now it's time to demonstrate your commitment to yourself, to changing your life through Coaching and to following the path of courage, determination and fearlessness by signing the contract below.

COACHING CONTRACT

I agree to demonstrate my commitment to myself and to the coaching relationship by:

1) Spending a minimum of 30 minutes a day, which I will set aside in advance, reading and working with this book.
2) Carrying out the challenges and assignments that my Coach sets for me – without delay.
3) Being willing to suspend my disbelief when necessary.

4) Agreeing to keep going, even when the going gets tough.
5) Choosing to adopt a more enthusiastic, optimistic perspective on my life from this moment onwards.

Signed   Date

I agree to coach you to the very best of my ability, to believe in you, to encourage you and to give you 100 percent of my energy and commitment.

Signed   *Fiona Harrold*   Date

By signing this contract with me you have made a bold and brave step towards becoming the person you want to be and creating the future you want to live. Congratulations and welcome aboard!

CHAPTER TWO

WHO DO YOU THINK YOU ARE? AND WHO DO YOU NEED TO THINK YOU ARE TO HAVE THE LIFE YOU WANT?

IN THIS chapter I will guide you through the very first steps towards achieving the goals and dreams that you have for your life. In order to be the best that you can be and to create the brilliant life that you deserve, it's necessary to start by understanding the way you see yourself. The greatest advantage you can have in life is to view yourself as special and to appreciate what those qualities are that distinguish you from every other person.

When you believe in yourself 100 percent, when you have the highest possible regard for yourself and expect to be able to create a positive, successful life for yourself then anything becomes possible. Sadly, very few people see themselves in this way. Most people are far more willing to list their bad qualities and weaknesses than their good ones and their strengths. And this is the way they limit their potential and create frustration and failure in their lives. Henry Ford summed this up nicely when he said: 'Whether you think you can or think you can't, you're usually right.'

Many people also feel that they have the ability to succeed in certain areas of their lives, but not in others. For instance, you may see yourself as being great at your job but hopeless in personal relationships. Or you may believe you can have a wonderful relationship, but that you can't be wealthy or powerful as well. But no matter how negative, unflattering or inadequate your picture of yourself, it is entirely possible, within a short space of time, to turn it around and become truly special in your own eyes. It is simply never too late to become the person you want to be.

This is the first gift I want you to give yourself. By the time you have finished this chapter you will be a star in your own eyes, a natural high achiever who consistently attracts luck and success in every area of your life. Together we are going to bring your self-image into line with the way you want your life to be, because your self-image is the foundation upon which your life is built. If you want a happy, successful, abundant life then you must see yourself as happy, successful, talented and lucky person. Your self-image is your blueprint for success and will determine every aspect of your life, from the way you feel about yourself to the quality of your relationships and the job you are doing.

This is why I am focusing on your self-image at the beginning of our journey together. The goals you are pursuing, the dreams you have are far less likely to be achieved if your self-image is poor. Once you have a strong, healthy self-image in place then everything else will become easier and more straightforward.

Natalie's story
A close friend of mine, Natalie, has one of the most powerful, positive self-images I've ever come across. Natalie's parents desperately wanted a child, and even though doctors warned her mother that having a child

WOULD ENDANGER HER LIFE, SHE WENT AHEAD AND FELL PREGNANT. THE PREGNANCY WAS GREETED WITH TREMENDOUS JOY AND CELEBRATION AND, ALTHOUGH SHE SPENT MOST OF HER PREGNANCY IN HOSPITAL, NATALIE'S MOTHER FELT IT WAS WORTH IT. ALL THE DOCTORS AND NURSES AT THE HOSPITAL COULD SEE HOW VERY SPECIAL THIS BABY WAS TO HER PARENTS, AND FELT THAT SHE WAS SPECIAL TOO.

SO NATALIE CAME INTO THE WORLD WITH A GREAT MANY PEOPLE ALREADY BELIEVING THAT SHE WAS PHENOMENALLY SPECIAL AND SHE GREW UP WITH THIS BELIEF FIRMLY IN PLACE IN HER OWN MIND. BECAUSE OF THIS NATALIE WAS QUIETLY CONFIDENT AND EXCITED ABOUT LIFE FROM A VERY YOUNG AGE. SHE TOOK IT FOR GRANTED THAT SHE WAS DESTINED TO LEAD A UNIQUE LIFE AND ONLY EVER ANTICIPATED SUCCESS AND FULFILMENT.

NATALIE HAS FULFILLED ALL THESE EXPECTATIONS. SHE IS NOW A BUBBLY, LIGHT-HEARTED 35-YEAR-OLD — A HIGHLY SUCCESSFUL TELEVISION PRODUCER AND AN IMMENSELY ATTRACTIVE, CHARISMATIC PERSON WHO IS A DELIGHT TO ALL WHO KNOW HER. SHE LEADS WHAT IS FREQUENTLY DESCRIBED AS A 'CHARMED LIFE'. SHE HAS A NATURAL RESILIENCE THAT ALLOWS HER TO BOUNCE BACK FROM SETBACKS AND DISAPPOINTMENTS AND SHE MOVES THROUGH LIFE WITH A LIGHT TOUCH, ATTRACTING THE RIGHT PEOPLE AND OPPORTUNITIES.

AS A CHILD NATALIE WAS LOVED AND CHERISHED BY EVERYONE AROUND HER. SO HOW COULD SHE FAIL TO SEE HERSELF AS SPECIAL? THIS DOESN'T MEAN, BY THE WAY, THAT SHE SEES HERSELF AS SUPERIOR TO ANYONE ELSE OR THAT SHE'S SMUG AND ARROGANT. THESE CHARACTERISTICS ALWAYS BELONG TO PEOPLE WHO ACTUALLY FEEL BAD ABOUT THEMSELVES. NATALIE SIMPLY HAS A HEALTHY APPRECIATION OF HER QUALITIES AND TALENTS AND A NATURAL CONFIDENCE THAT CARRIES HER THROUGH LIFE.

THE ORIGINS OF YOUR SELF-IMAGE

I want you to see yourself in exactly the same way that Natalie does. I want the unnecessary difficulty and struggle removed from your life and replaced with ease and success and I am going to show you how you can achieve this.

Does this all sound a bit far-fetched? Are you convinced that the person you are is simply the person you are, determined by genes, birth and circumstance and impossible to change? Many people feel this way. Jennifer, a good friend and a forward-thinking, bright woman told me that 'everyone has their own level'. She felt that we are all predisposed to an inbuilt level of achievement.

My belief and my experience is that we simply find the level in life that we are conditioned to find and that we are led to expect. The current self-image you have is the result of the repeated messages and instructions you received as a child from the authority figures in your world. The way you see yourself today is the result of conditioning by your parents, family, teachers and other influential adults and peers in your life.

The saying 'give me the boy until he is seven and I will show you the man' is true. Each one of us is powerfully programmed to be a certain way, to have certain beliefs and to take certain actions.

This theory was brought home to me recently by a conversation I had with an eight-year-old friend of my son's. I was giving Andrew a lift home from school and asked him what he would like to be when he grows up.

'Oh, I don't know. I'll work in a shop, I suppose,' he told me.

'That's interesting,' I replied. 'Any particular type of shop?'

'No,' he answered. 'Just whatever one pays the most.'

Andrew asked what Jamie, my ten-year-old, wanted to do.

'He wants to be a pop star and, most importantly, to have a stretch limo as soon as possible,' I told him.

'Pah, he's a dreamer,' Andrew scoffed. 'Only a few people can be pop stars and stretch limos cost a lot of money.'

Clearly Andrew has not been conditioned to look forward to a compelling future! There is absolutely nothing wrong with working in a shop, but the way this child spoke about it told me that he saw himself as someone who could only aspire to work in a shop. For him, working in a shop was not an exciting choice but something he felt someone like him would end up doing.

Already, at the age of eight, Andrew has a self-image in place that is enormously restricting. Unless he is lucky enough to be exposed to a very different kind of adult influence he is going to be condemned to a life where his stock answer to challenging ideas is *Pah*. And, of course, by the time he is an adult he will have accumulated enormous amounts of evidence, as we all do, to support his particular attitude to life. He'll have all kinds of reasons and justifications to prove why anything beyond the life he has isn't possible. His self-image will ensure that he will never lead an extraordinary life and he is likely to be a cynic with a *pah* attitude that makes him bitter and resentful of anyone else's success.

The only way to change childhood conditioning like this is to make the decision to be in charge of your own programming and to re-programme those thoughts and beliefs that hold you back.

Your life to date is the result of your past beliefs. Your future will be the result of the beliefs you choose to hold today. You are shaping your future, right now. It will be your choice to live a life of conventional limitation and miniscule potential or a life of unlimited opportunities and infinite possibilities.

Your self-image is no more fixed and absolute than what you will have for breakfast tomorrow. You could wake up and decide to have champagne and peaches instead of tea and toast. Well, your self-image is the same. Decide today that you're going to upgrade it to the very highest level, because this is the choice you have. You have the ability and the choice, right now, to exceed all your previous levels of accomplishment.

THE SELF-IMAGE YOU HAVE RIGHT NOW

It's time to dig a little deeper and find out about the way you see yourself right now. The key to unlocking your potential is to understand what you have learned to think and feel about yourself so far in your life. With that understanding comes the ability to change and to choose new ways of thinking and behaving, which will result in more positive feelings about yourself.

The way you think about yourself determines everything you say, do, believe and feel. The world around you is a reflection of your inner world. Whatever you see outside you has a parallel inside you. For instance, if you believe that you are not very physically attractive then your external world will confirm this internal belief. In other words, you'll notice and collect evidence which supports it, such as a criticism of your looks, while deflecting or ignoring anything which doesn't match your belief, such as a compliment. So the burning question is, who do you think you are?

EXERCISE

Take a pen and paper and answer the following question in no more than ten lines. Don't think or plan, just write whatever comes into your mind.

Who do I think I am?

What you'll have noticed, doing this, is that you have all sorts of thoughts and conclusions about yourself – a mixture of good and bad, positive and negative.

Some of these thoughts will, of course, be appropriate and useful in your life. But the ones I'm interested in are the ones that get in the way of your dreams and hopes, and hold you back. Living with these kinds of negative thoughts about yourself is like travelling through life with the brakes on. You may reach some of your destinations, but getting there will be an uphill battle, demanding effort and struggle. And other destinations will remain impossibly out of reach. It is likely that the negative thoughts and beliefs you have about yourself centre on one or two particular areas of your life. Most of us have different self-images for different parts of our lives and I often find with new clients that one part of their life is functioning just fine while another isn't working at all.

JONATHAN'S STORY

JONATHAN WAS A CLIENT OF MINE WHO HAD A SUPERB SELF–IMAGE AROUND HIS WORK AND CAREER. HE WAS BRILLIANT AT HIS JOB, REGULARLY AND EFFORTLESSLY GAINING PROMOTION. BUT WHEN IT CAME TO WOMEN AND FINDING A GOOD RELATIONSHIP IT WAS A VERY DIFFERENT MATTER.

JONATHAN WAS LONGING TO MEET THE RIGHT WOMAN AND SETTLE DOWN. HE'D JOINED A DATING AGENCY AND GONE ON A NUMBER OF DATES, ALL WITH VERY LIMITED SUCCESS. DURING OUR FIRST CONSULTATION I FORBADE HIM TO GO ON ANY MORE DATES FOR AT LEAST A MONTH, BECAUSE UNTIL HIS SELF–IMAGE AROUND WOMEN AND RELATIONSHIPS WAS CHANGED, THERE WAS SIMPLY NO POINT. HE HAD TO DO THE GROUNDWORK IN ORDER TO FIND SUCCESS.

JONATHAN AND I SOON DISCOVERED THAT HE SAW HIMSELF AS SOMEONE WHO ATTRACTED WOMEN WHO LET HIM DOWN. HE BELIEVED HE WAS LUCKY TO HAVE A GIRLFRIEND AT ALL. THIS WAS CLEARLY A DISASTROUS POSITION FROM WHICH TO OPERATE.

JONATHAN WAS ABLE TO SEE THAT HE PUT HIS GIRLFRIENDS ON PEDESTALS, A POSITION THAT THEY NEITHER ASKED FOR NOR DESERVED. HE SAW HIS GIRLFRIENDS AS TERRIFICALLY VALUABLE AND

HIMSELF AS THEIR ADMIRER. IN HIS LAST RELATIONSHIP HE HAD INVESTED HUGE AMOUNTS OF TIME AND ENERGY HELPING HIS GIRLFRIEND TO LOSE WEIGHT, REGAIN HER CONFIDENCE AND GET HER LIFE BACK ON TRACK. SO HE WAS LEFT FEELING TERRIBLY SHORT-CHANGED AND DISAPPOINTED WHEN SHE FAILED TO GIVE HIM THE SAME KIND OF DEVOTION IN RETURN.

I ENCOURAGED JONATHAN TO WORK INTENSIVELY TO REPLACE HIS LOW SELF-IMAGE WITH A FRESH ONE IN WHICH HE SAW HIMSELF AS THE KIND OF MAN WHO NATURALLY ATTRACTED TERRIFIC, TRUSTWORTHY WOMEN. HE WOULD SELL HIMSELF AS THE TYPE OF GUY THAT ANY WOMAN WOULD BE LUCKY TO HAVE IN HER LIFE. WITHIN A SHORT TIME JONATHAN'S CONFIDENCE LEVELS SOARED. HIS FRIENDS NOTICED THAT HE HAD BECOME MORE CONFIDENT AND OUTGOING AND HE FELT READY TO TRY DATING AGAIN.

JONATHAN FOUND HE WAS ABLE TO WALK AWAY FROM UNSUITABLE WOMEN BECAUSE HE HAD SET NEW STANDARDS FOR HIMSELF AND WAS NO LONGER WILLING TO BE TREATED BADLY. WITHIN WEEKS HE MET A LOVELY WOMAN AND HE'S NOW VERY HAPPY WITH HER AND ENJOYING A COMPLETELY NEW KIND OF RELATIONSHIP.

EXERCISE

Let's dig a little deeper and find out what you learned about yourself from your earliest authority figures: your parents, teachers and other close adults. Take a pen and a notebook and write five answers to each of the following questions:

1) *Something I learned about myself from my mother was . . .*
2) *Something I learned about myself from my father was . . .*
3) *Something I learned about myself from school was . . .*
4) *Something I learned about myself from (put in another early authority figure here) was . . .*

Do some of your answers appear more than once? Do you instantly recognise the more familiar ones? Can you see clearly which statements are the chief culprits in restricting you and holding you back?

Perhaps you received very different messages from each parent. This is very common and often causes confusion and uncertainty. Perhaps writing this information down has been revealing and sparked off all kinds of memories for you. If you feel the need to talk about or work through any of these insights then do find a good listener, a friend or perhaps a professional counsellor.

My interest in your past is simply to see how it is affecting you now and may affect your future. My approach does not involve focusing on the past because my objective is to move you forward with momentum and enthusiasm, and as quickly as possible. To focus on the past at length will only deflect us from this goal.

EXERCISE

Take pen and paper again and complete the following statement with the first ten answers that come to mind:

> *The limiting beliefs I hold about myself are . . .*
> Do the same for this statement
> *The three limiting beliefs that hold me back most of all are . . .*

With the responses to these statements you now have all the information you need about the most damaging and restrictive ways in which you see yourself. Those three key beliefs, in particular, have a powerful influence over the way you shape your life. And when you choose to change these beliefs then you are no longer at the mercy of your conditioning.

SUZANNE'S STORY

SUZANNE WAS AN IMMENSELY WARM, LIKEABLE 40-YEAR-OLD WHO'D

RECENTLY BEEN DIVORCED AND WAS BRINGING UP TWO CHILDREN ON HER OWN. SHE WAS ALSO GOING BACK TO WORK IN RECRUITMENT CONSULTING AFTER TEN YEARS AS A FULL-TIME MUM.

WHEN I BEGAN COACHING SUZANNE IT QUICKLY BECAME EVIDENT THAT SHE SAW HERSELF AS BEING ESSENTIALLY STUPID. HER PROGRAMMING WAS SO POWERFUL AND SO ENTRENCHED THAT HER BEHAVIOUR AT WORK WAS COMPLETELY COLOURED BY THIS CONVICTION. SHE HAD VERY LITTLE FAITH IN HER ABILITY TO CARRY OUT SIMPLE TASKS AND SHE FREQUENTLY FORGOT OR MISLAID TELEPHONE NUMBERS.

WHEN I POINTED OUT TO SUZANNE THAT SHE TALKED AND BEHAVED AS THOUGH SHE BELIEVED HERSELF TO BE STUPID, SHE AGREED. SHE TOLD ME THAT SHE HAD BEEN BELITTLED THROUGHOUT HER CHILDHOOD AND HAD THEN MARRIED AN OVERBEARING MAN WHO HAD ONLY CONFIRMED HER BELIEF IN HER OWN STUPIDITY. ONCE SHE UNDERSTOOD WHAT HAD HAPPENED SUZANNE BEGAN TO CONSCIOUSLY REJECT AND CHANGE THIS RIDICULOUS BUT LONG-HELD VIEW OF HERSELF. WE WERE ABLE TO LAUGH AT THE BELIEF SHE'D BEEN HARBOURING LIKE A DARK SECRET, AND THIS INSTANTLY DIMINISHED ITS POWER.

AS SUZANNE REPLACED IT WITH NEW, POSITIVE AND POWERFUL BELIEFS SHE BECAME MORE CONFIDENT. SOON SHE WAS MUCH LESS AFRAID OF MAKING MISTAKES, SHE WAS MORE WILLING TO TAKE RISKS, AND FOUND THAT SHE ENJOYED BEING CLEVER AND WELL-ORGANISED. SHE WAS SURPRISED THAT CHANGE COULD COME ABOUT SO EASILY AND SO FAST AND THAT A BELIEF THAT HAD DOMINATED HER LIFE COULD BE SO EFFECTIVELY PUT BEHIND HER.

EXERCISE

Before we move on to your new self-image I want you to do just one more exercise. I want you to notice and understand just how much your limiting beliefs have cost you so far. After that you'll certainly be ready to leave them behind!

Take a pen and paper and write five responses to the following statement:

The cost to me, in my life, of my limiting beliefs is . . .

Realising how much your beliefs may have cost you can be disappointing. Think of the jobs or relationships you may have missed, the excitement and fulfilment of achievements you could have had, the opportunities you passed by or failed to recognise. But don't dwell on these disappointments. You're about to move on to wonderful new opportunities, so don't hesitate for longer than a sobering moment. It's time to let go of the past and to begin building your future.

THE NEW YOU

It's time now to redefine yourself according to the way you want to see yourself and to be seen by others. You are about to become someone who is self-made and to reject any outdated or damaging beliefs that were dumped on you by others. You will be the person you choose to be, a person you like and admire and love being. This doesn't mean you're going to be someone entirely different, because there are lots of qualities you'll want to keep. It just means you're shedding the stuff you no longer need and creating a stronger, healthier more successful you who has an easier, more enjoyable life.

EXERCISE

Write down the seven qualities you most admire in other people. Look at friends, family, and even people you've never met or who have impressed you at a single meeting. Think about the attributes that attracted you and made you like them.

Now think about yourself and the qualities you would most like to be known for. Imagine you were the topic of conversation at a dinner party. What would you like people to be saying about you?

For instance, might you like to be referred to as a straightforward person who treats everyone with the same grace; someone who is consistently cheerful and great to be around? Or someone who seems to have amazing good luck, with a knack of being in the right place at the right time?

YOUR MISSION STATEMENT

Take your pen and paper and complete these statements:

1) *The person I am choosing to be from this day on is someone who is . . .*
2) *The qualities I most want to emphasise and enjoy in myself are . . .*

Once you have finished, add the following statement beneath:

3) *I am now ready to give life to this new image of myself, from this day forth. I commit to reinforcing these qualities until they are a deeply ingrained part of who I am and who I am seen to be.*

Sign and date your statement underneath and keep it in a place where you will see it often.

This is your own personal mission statement. From now on your behaviour, choices and decisions should always fit this description of you. When you are faced with a choice or a decision ask yourself: 'What is the answer, given the person I am now?'

BREATHING LIFE INTO THE NEW YOU

So, you've chosen the qualities you wish to have, you know how you want to be perceived by others and how you want to feel about yourself. The next step is to become so familiar and comfortable with your new characteristics and attributes that they are a part of you and have simply replaced the old characteristics you discarded.

Making this change and learning to look at yourself is simply a question of learning new habits. And with all new habits the way to make them part of your life is to reinforce and practise them. And there are simple techniques that will help you to do this.

Refine your internal dialogue

Your subconscious mind has been successfully programmed by simple, repeated instructions and messages from others around you. As a result, certain beliefs have been created. In order to replace these old beliefs with new ones you must do the same thing; in other words, reprogramme. This time *you* will choose the instructions and messages and *you* will give them to your subconscious mind.

The way to do this is through simple, repeated statements. For instance, if you have always seen yourself as someone who is naturally overweight and will always be overweight, you might try statements like:

It is natural for me to be slim, I now move easily towards my ideal weight. I choose to eat light, nutritious food, I respect my body and give it only the best.

These positive statements are called affirmations. Repeated frequently they create powerful new messages for your subconscious to absorb. Give yourself these messages as often as you can, dozens or even hundreds of times a day – because that's how often you have the opposite, negative thoughts. Write your affirmations out and pin them up where you can see them; say them out loud when you can; look in the mirror and say them to yourself.

It doesn't matter, at this stage, whether you believe them or not. Remember, you are creating new beliefs, so suspend your doubts and be totally disciplined about thinking only the highest quality thoughts. As Wayne Dyer, the brilliant motivational speaker says: 'You are what you think about all day long.'

Here are some other affirmations. You can choose to use any or all of these, or to create your own.

- *I like myself.*
- *I now take responsibility for making my life work.*
- *My future is full of interesting surprises and wonderful opportunities.*
- *I am good enough.*
- *I now know I deserve to have more fun, laughter, money and success.*
- *I approve of myself completely, including in the presence of others.*
- *I now choose to like and trust myself and to treat myself with the utmost respect.*

Refine your external dialogue

Who you say you are is confirmed by the way you speak about yourself. So it's vital that you give up self-deprecating, belittling and apologetic ways of talking about yourself right now. These are among the most common ways to trip yourself up and fail to create your new self-image. When I talk to clients I correct them rigorously on this point, because the only purpose this type of talking serves is to slow them down and put obstacles in their way.

The kinds of phrases I'm thinking of include:

- *Trust me to get it wrong.*
- *Knowing my luck it will be too late.*

- *I'm only a . . .*
- *I wish I could but there's no chance.*
- *I'm not very good at this sort of thing.*
- *I never win anything.*
- *I've got a memory like a sieve.*
- *I never could add up.*
- *I hope I can manage it.*

I'm sure you can add your own phrases to this list. Watch out, in particular, for the word 'sorry', which crops up an awful lot in apology-speak. Please promise me, and yourself, that you will give up self-deprecating talk right now.

This kind of talk is neither harmless nor meaningless. It is a highly effective method of reinforcing destructive ways of thinking and looking at yourself. The way you speak will define you and if you talk this way people will instantly know that you have a low opinion of yourself. So eradicate this kind of talk and replace it with strong, confident statements which indicate that you like and believe in yourself.

SEE AND FEEL YOUR SUCCESS

The technique of visualisation has been used for centuries as a powerful means of training the human mind, and it is a wonderful tool to use in bringing about change. Visualising literally means 'seeing' in your mind's eye, the scene that you want to create. To reinforce your new behaviour and the new you, create pictures for yourself of the events you want to bring about.

How many times have you heard people say things like: 'I just can't picture that,' 'I can't see myself doing that', and 'I can't envisage that scenario'?

To talk in this way is to shut out the possibility of that particular scenario ever coming true. It's vital to envisage regularly the scenarios you want, particularly first thing in the morning and last thing at night. Before you go to sleep, and again in the morning, picture your coming day's events and see yourself moving effortlessly and successfully through the day. See people responding in exactly the way you would wish. Feel the atmosphere, hear and smell what is going on around you. It's a remarkable, powerful way of preparing yourself for success. There's a saying that goes: 'If you can dream it you can believe it and if you believe it you can achieve it.'

ALICE'S STORY

ALICE HAD RECENTLY MOVED FROM NEW YORK TO A VERY EXCLUSIVE VILLAGE IN HAMPSHIRE. SHE WAS LIVING IN A MODERN-DAY *VANITY FAIR* WHERE TO BE INVITED TO THE RIGHT DINNER PARTIES AND LUNCHES WAS EVERYTHING. ALICE FOUND THE SNOBBERY AND GOSSIP INTIMIDATING, BUT WAS DETERMINED NOT TO SIT AT HOME. SHE PLANNED TO SOCIALISE IN THE HOPE OF MEETING LIKE-MINDED PEOPLE.

SHE CAME TO ME A WEEK BEFORE THE BALL OF THE SEASON, DETERMINED TO ATTEND AND TO ENJOY HERSELF. SHE ASKED ME TO HELP HER MAKE AN IMPRESSION. SHE WANTED TO BE ABLE TO MAKE A GRAND ENTRANCE AND TO HAVE EVERY HEAD TURN WHEN SHE WALKED INTO THE ROOM.

I ASKED ALICE WHY SHE WANTED THIS AND WE BEGAN TO LOOK A LITTLE DEEPER AT WHAT SHE WANTED FROM THE EVENING. ALICE REALISED THAT WHAT SHE ACTUALLY WANTED WAS TO FEEL RELAXED, COMPLETELY COMFORTABLE WITH HERSELF AND AT EASE SOCIALLY.

I ASKED ALICE TO CLOSE HER EYES AND TO PICTURE HERSELF MOVING SEAMLESSLY THROUGH THE EVENING'S EVENTS, EFFORTLESSLY

MAKING CONVERSATION, MOVING ON QUICKLY AND POLITELY FROM
THE PEOPLE SHE FELT DAUNTED BY AND FEELING WONDERFUL ABOUT
HERSELF THROUGHOUT. WE MENTALLY REHEARSED EVERY ASPECT OF
THE EVENING.

I SUGGESTED SHE REPLAY THIS SCENARIO TO HERSELF A FEW MORE
TIMES BEFORE THE BALL, WHICH SHE DID. AS I EXPECTED,
EVERYTHING WENT JUST AS ALICE HAD PLANNED AND PICTURED IT.
SHE CALLED ME TO SAY SHE HAD RELAXED, FELT COMFORTABLE AND
ABLE TO SPOT THE MORE INTERESTING PEOPLE, AND HAD MANAGED
TO AVOID FEELING UNDERMINED BY OTHERS.

ACT THE PART

A simple and brilliant way to enhance your new self image is to act
the part of the person you want to be. Doing this you will notice
immediate results.

All you have to do is consciously adopt the self-image you have
chosen and behave as though you already were that person. This is
what method actors do all the time. Daniel Day Lewis takes this
role-playing so seriously that in order to portray Danny in the film
The Boxer he trained to the standard of a professional lightweight
champion. For the role of tortured prisoner Gerard Conlon in the
film *In the Name of the Father,* he went without food for days and
had buckets of cold water thrown over him.

Now I'm not suggesting you go to quite these extremes, but the
bottom line is that when you throw yourself into a part it becomes
real. You convince yourself deep down that you are that person
and in doing so you become that person.

You can test the truth of this by smiling next time you see
someone, whether you feel cheerful or not. The response you get,
both physiologically in your own body and from the other person,
will immediately make you feel more cheerful.

ANTHONY'S STORY

ANTHONY WAS PARTICULARLY ANXIOUS NOT TO LET HIS NERVOUSNESS SPOIL A DATE HE HAD ARRANGED WITH A NEW GIRLFRIEND. HE WAS GETTING INTO SUCH A STATE ABOUT IT THAT HE WAS BEGINNING TO DREAD THE EVENING INSTEAD OF LOOKING FORWARD TO IT.

IT TOOK ONLY A FEW MINUTES TO TURN HIS FEELINGS AROUND SO THAT HE FELT EXCITED AND OPTIMISTIC. HOW DID WE DO THIS? I SIMPLY ASKED ANTHONY TO DEFINE WHO HE WOULD NEED TO BE IN ORDER TO RELAX AND ENJOY THE EVENING. ANTHONY DECIDED HE WOULD NEED TO BE SOMEONE WHO FELT COMPLETELY COMFORTABLE WITH HIMSELF, WHO LIKED HIMSELF, SMILED OFTEN, ENJOYED OTHER PEOPLE'S COMPANY AND HAD A GENUINE INTEREST IN OTHERS, WHO FELT AT EASE IN NEW SITUATIONS AND WHO HAD A KNACK OF PUTTING PEOPLE AT EASE INSTANTLY. ALL ANTHONY HAD TO DO WAS TO GO ON HIS DATE BEHAVING AS THOUGH HE WAS THIS PERSON. THE RESULT? HE WENT OUT FEELING RELAXED AND SPONTANEOUS AND HAD A TERRIFIC EVENING.

YOUR ASSIGNMENT

From this moment on I want you to breathe life into this new, upgraded self-image you have chosen. I want you to use the tools and techniques I have outlined in this chapter and to take total charge of your mental habits and your behaviour. Back yourself 100 percent and accept nothing less. Be the best you can be, at all times. The Royal Marines' slogan is: '*You can slow down, but you can't stop.*' *When you falter get right back up again, stronger and more determined than ever. Don't let yourself down because you deserve to be the best.*

So dream, believe and take action. You are on your way.

AND REMEMBER . . .

When you believe in yourself anything is possible.

  Any beliefs which hold you back must be discarded.

  Until you see yourself as successful no one else will see you that way.

  Choose to see yourself as a happy, successful, talented and lucky person.

  Act, talk and behave like the person you want to be and you will become that person.

CHAPTER THREE

How To Unleash Your Personal Power: Exude Glowing Self-confidence and Build a Magnetic Personality

HIGH LEVELS of self-worth and self-confidence are vital to a happy, successful life. They are the blocks with which you will build a hard core of self-belief. Strong self-belief, self-generated security and internal resources are what separate Masters from the masses, exceptional human beings from the average and charismatic leaders from followers.

In today's world your security comes from being a Master. Mastery is rooted in indestructible self-belief, which in turn brings serenity, security, self-acceptance and a profound sense of comfort and ease within yourself, which is intriguing, irresistible and compelling to others.

In this chapter I want to define self-worth, to look at why it is often so low in many individuals and to show you what you can do to generate and sustain deep-rooted regard and esteem for yourself. Everything you attract into your life is a reflection of what you feel you deserve, what you feel you are worth and how highly you value yourself in all areas of life. The opportunities, the people, the breaks and the luck you attract are all a direct result of the messages you are sending out. The circumstances of your life – personal, professional and social – tell you everything about how you rate yourself.

So what is self-worth and where does it come from? My definition is simple: *self-worth is the degree to which you like yourself.*

We are all born with strong self-worth. It is a given, in the nature of being human. Yet somehow, along the way to adulthood, most of us end up with our stock of it severely depleted. And when this happens, because we need to feel good about ourselves and to feel valued and valuable, we begin looking outside ourselves for self-worth and to expect others to give it to us.

This is where we go wrong, because true self-worth can only be self-generated. It can't be conferred on you by anyone or anything else. It is not determined by peer approval, economic status or cultural success. True self-worth is a sense of internal composure that gives you complete freedom. When you have it your life choices will spring from genuine desires and talents, rather than a need to achieve or impress.

Life today offers very little external security or certainty, so it is more vital than ever that you find safety from within. And this is the route I urge you to take at this juncture. I will outline the steps you need to take in order to have phenomenally high self-worth, which will give you an internal sense of peace and safety and carry you effortlessly through life. Make the choice to do the work, make the changes and go for high self-worth and I will be cheering you along the way.

A conversation I overheard recently between two friends illustrates perfectly the difference between a person with high self-worth and someone without it.

Hilary was bemoaning the fact that, at almost thirty, she had never been proposed to, while her friend Janice had received and turned down numerous proposals. I know both women and to me there was no mystery at all about why this was the case. Quite simply, Janice is someone who prizes herself and who sees herself as a prize worth having and winning. Only the very best, most suitable man will do for her. It's easy to see that Janice feels great about herself. She always looks fabulous, she takes terrific care of herself with the best food, regular exercise and health and beauty treatments. Janice takes pride in her appearance and in herself, too. She puts herself on a pedestal and everyone follows her cue, especially the men she attracts.

Hilary, on the other hand, has had a stream of disappointing relationships. She blames herself for making poor choices when it comes to boyfriends and feels grateful to have a boyfriend at all. Men invariably pick up on this and treat her with little thought or courtesy. Her personal appearance also gives the message that she does not rate looking after herself as a major priority. Hilary's problem is not her boyfriends but the message she gives them about how to treat her. Take the same man and he will be two different people, depending on whether he's with Hilary or Janice.

THE ORIGINS OF LOW SELF-WORTH

My experience of working with clients over the years is that very few people enjoy a high level of personal comfort and ease. On the contrary, in most cases the slightest probing reveals that most people don't like themselves very much at all.

And this state of self-dislike often begins very young. I recently had a conversation with Alastair, a nine-year-old friend of my son's. Alastair was convinced that Jamie didn't like him any more and that most of his classmates didn't like him either.

I replied, 'But Alastair, the important thing here is, do you like yourself?'

Without hesitation he replied emphatically, 'No, definitely not.' I was absolutely astounded and very saddened that, at nine, he already felt so bad about himself.

Alastair was saying exactly the same thing as countless men and women I've spoken to over the years. He simply put it more clearly and simply than many adults, who might never ask themselves the question, 'Do I like me?'

This fundamental lack of self-regard and self-respect cuts through all social and educational divides, undermining even the most outwardly confident and successful people. Symptoms of low self-worth are rife. Among the most extreme are eating disorders. The most famous sufferer was Diana, Princess of Wales, who drew the world's attention to the 'invisible' problem of bulimia and brilliantly explained the link between low self-esteem and eating disorders.

Women, men and even children as young as five are increasingly affected by these disorders. And the problem is made far worse by the rigid cultural role models of skinny women offered to us by the media. We are continually told that only individuals with a specific body type can be beautiful and there is no variation on this theme. There are very few more varied, attainable role models of health and beauty.

Highly impressionable young children, girls in particular, are given painfully thin pop stars and models as role models and told that these are the beautiful people who have made it and who led exciting, glamorous lives. Young girls are pressured into seeing body shape as the route to valuing oneself and being valued. The result is that half of all girls aged fifteen to sixteen are not happy with their weight and one in four is on a diet. On top of this one in three fifteen-year-old girls has started smoking – a habit that is always associated with low self-esteem, while drinking alcohol, another low self-esteem habit, is higher among eighteen to 24-year-old women than for any other age group. Another relatively new low self-esteem condition, body dysmorphic disorder, is also increasing at an alarming rate. Sufferers see themselves as hideously ugly and freak-like and often stay indoors to avoid being seen. In Britain alone it is currently estimated that 600,000 people suffer from this condition and the true figure may be much higher.

Western culture, Christian teaching and, in many cases, parental conditioning all taught us as children that to think well of ourselves and feel good about ourselves is vain, selfish and wrong. We were encouraged to develop the qualities of humility and meekness, in order to be good people. Even those of us whose families were not actively religious will have received these messages through our culture. The British are characterised the world over for their bumbling charm, their modesty, their shyness and their inability to receive compliments or accept credit for their achievements. The characters played by Hugh Grant in films such as *Nine Months, Four Weddings and a Funeral* and *Notting Hill* demonstrate this perfectly.

The American attitude, – that everyone is entitled to success and can be proud of it and that self-motivation, determination and ambition are worthwhile – is very different to the British one.

Most of us were trained to put the needs and desires of others above our own and to see ourselves as being less important than others. We were taught that the way to win love and approval was to put the needs of others first and to be modest and self-deprecating at all times. Women, in particular, are still conditioned to be the primary carers, highly attuned to the needs of others.

Think of common sayings that confirm this attitude: 'Stop blowing your own trumpet', 'Don't be so big-headed', 'You're too big for your boots', 'You're too full of yourself', or 'Self-praise is no praise'. The list goes on and on.

Of course many of us are making sure that things are different for today's children. My style of parenting with my son Jamie, differs greatly from that of my mother's generation. I take every opportunity to encourage him to take pride in himself to see himself as intrinsically brilliant and special and to believe that he is someone who can do anything to which he puts his mind. He has been fed a diet of massive appreciation, lots of physical contact, constant praise and love.

As a baby he always drew admiring comments about his blue eyes and cute face, which thrilled me enormously. I took great pride in him and always heartily agreed with whoever complimented him. Older friends were surprised by my open enthusiasm and encouraged me to be grateful and to smile coyly instead. They suggested that I might spoil him by cuddling him too much or make him big-headed with too much praise and encouragement. That's just the sort of parenting that previous generations said would spoil a child and guarantee to turn him into a monster.

Yet Jamie, at nine, is now one of the kindest and most loving human beings you could ever meet. I have watched him hand over his precious pocket money to a beggar and he is remarkably attuned to others' needs and qualities. The attitude was, and often still is, that if children are encouraged to think of themselves as special they will grow up to be intolerable adults, vain, selfish and arrogant, seeing themselves as superior and everyone else as less worthy.

The truth is that only when we have been fed huge amounts of appreciation, love and generosity as children and taught to like ourselves that we can be free to extend the same appreciation, love and generosity to others. People who are brought up to like and feel good about themselves become happier, more successful, kinder and nicer people. It's that simple.

EXERCISE

Please run through this exercise without pausing or agonising. The answers are not hidden away, you know them without even having to think. Let's just get them nailed down on paper now. Keep them brief and don't worry if you repeat any of them.

Answer the following questions:

1) *How do I rate my self-worth now (on a scale from 0 to 100)?*
2) *If my rate is less than 100 the three reasons why this is so are:*
3) *What exactly stops me from liking myself more?*
4) *What are three ways that I hold myself back through not having enough belief in myself?*
5) *What are three things that I do to be liked by others and feel likeable?*
6) *What three things do I tolerate/put up with in my life?*
7) *For what three things do I blame or resent myself?*
8) *For what three things will I not forgive myself?*
9) *In what three ways do I punish myself?*

For instance, I found I was tolerating a friend who was always very late and kept me waiting. I told her that I cared about her, but that my time was precious and I didn't want to spend it waiting for her. After that she turned up on time. Something I blamed myself for was hurting my parents when I was a teenager. I chose to forgive myself for this, and felt much better for letting it go.

The answers you have given will provide you with a good MOT report on the current condition of your self-worth. My priority now – and yours, I hope – is to improve your opinion of yourself so that you like yourself more and see yourself in the best possible light.

THE FEELGOOD FACTOR

A state of being in which you genuinely like yourself and are profoundly at ease with yourself and able to generate immense enthusiasm and optimism for life contains what I call the 'feelgood factor'. We are all looking for this feelgood factor, and most of us look for it outside ourselves. The need for it gnaws away at us and although it can be held at bay with compliments, a pay rise, a new car or a trophy girlfriend or boyfriend these things only ever bring temporary satisfaction. Until you really think about your life in this context, you won't know the extent to which you are driven by this need.

Without this feelgood factor that people like Janice (see page 41) exude, you will go through life without the support of the most constant, ever-present potential ally you will ever have . . . yourself. All of us come into the world on our own and we leave on our own. At some point in between it makes sense to get comfortable with ourselves. So, making peace with yourself, getting comfortable in your own skin on your own terms, befriending yourself and backing yourself 100 percent throughout life is the ultimate and only route to internal security and external optimism.

EXERCISE

Ask yourself these questions right now:

1) *How much do I back myself in my life (on a scale from 0 to 100)?*
2) *If your score is less than 100, ask yourself why.*

The feelgood factor is like a safety net that allows you to follow your desires, take risks and lead the sort of life you want to live as opposed to the life that you or anyone else think you should live.

Without this safety net you will always be looking for security and status, approval and respect.

Your feelgood factor has nothing to do with arrogance or isolation. On the contrary, to take responsibility for your own happiness and to take steps to create the life you want is to show maturity and generosity. To upgrade your levels of self-worth and happiness is neither self-centred nor indulgent, and it will actually have a positive effect on all those around you. It is unhappy people with low self-worth who tend to be the most self-focused and who can be socially withdrawn, brooding and even antagonistic. Happy people, by contrast, are generally found to be more sociable, flexible and creative and are more able to tolerate life's frustrations. They are also more loving and forgiving, towards themselves and others.

There is a feeling of affinity and goodwill towards others that can only occur when we have taken care of ourselves and taken responsibility for generating our own happiness. Generosity of spirit flows from an internal spring of self-acceptance, self-respect and personal comfort. Generosity and 'bigness' of character can only flourish when we have provided for ourselves and have plenty over to share.

Thankfully we have enormous influence over this feelgood factor. It is never too late to re-educate yourself and to begin to build new levels of self-worth and self-belief, and I am going to take you through the steps that will lead you towards optimum self-worth and glowing self-confidence.

Exercise

Take a few minutes to answer the following question:

1) *How would my life be different if I really believed in myself?*

ANDREW'S STORY

ANDREW CAME TO ME AFTER THREE YEARS AS THE CEO OF A MAJOR COMPANY. HE ADMITTED THAT HE HAD NEVER FELT COMFORTABLE WITH HIS PROMOTION AND HE WORKED EXCESSIVELY LONG HOURS IN ORDER TO COMPENSATE FOR HIS PERCEIVED INADEQUACIES AND IN AN ATTEMPT TO CONVINCE HIS CHAIRMAN AND STAFF OF HIS ABILITIES.

ANDREW FELT LIKE AN IMPOSTER, WAITING FOR SOMEONE TO SPOT THAT HE JUST WASN'T UP TO THE JOB. HE ALSO REALISED THAT HE DOMINATED MEETINGS AND FELT HE ALWAYS HAD TO HAVE SOMETHING WITTY AND INTERESTING; HE WAS COMPELLED TO HAVE ALL THE ANSWERS AND, OF COURSE, THE LAST WORD.

ALL OF THIS WAS BECOMING AN INTOLERABLE STRAIN. THE TREMENDOUS STRESS HE WAS PUTTING HIMSELF UNDER HAD PLAYED HAVOC WITH HIS STOMACH AND HE HAD DEVELOPED IRRITABLE BOWEL SYNDROME (IBS). HE HAD ALSO GAINED TWO STONE IN WEIGHT THROUGH OVEREATING AND NEGLECTING HIS EXERCISE ROUTINE.

ONCE I HAD IDENTIFIED WHAT WAS DRIVING ANDREW — HIS FEAR OF FAILURE AND NEED TO BE LIKED BY EVERYONE — HE WAS ABLE TO PULL BACK AND BEGIN TO RELAX INTO BEING THE IMMENSELY CAPABLE PERSON HE ALREADY WAS. THE ONLY PERSON WHO HAD FAILED TO SEE HIS ABILITY WAS ANDREW HIMSELF.

WE WORKED WITH SPECIFIC NEW THOUGHTS AND BELIEFS TO REPLACE ALL THE TORTUOUS ONES HE HAD AND I ASKED HIM TO BE VIGILANT AND WATCH OUT FOR ALL THE FAMILIAR TELL-TALE SIGNS OF HIS OLD BEHAVIOUR THREATENING TO REAPPEAR. FOR ANDREW THE KEY WAS AWARENESS. ONCE HE UNDERSTOOD THAT HIS NEEDINESS WAS AT THE ROOT OF THE PROBLEM IT WAS SIMPLY A MATTER OF BOTH OF US MONITORING HIS BEHAVIOUR TO KEEP HIM MOVING FORWARD.

WITHIN A WEEK OF OUR FIRST CONSULTATION HE HAD DRAMATICALLY ALTERED HIS WORK SCHEDULE AND BEGAN TO CONDUCT HIMSELF LIKE SOMEONE WHO HAD NOTHING TO PROVE AND WHO WAS ENTIRELY COMFORTABLE WITH HIMSELF. HE WAS ABLE TO LEAVE WORK AT MORE REASONABLE TIMES, HE TOOK UP RUNNING AGAIN AND RETURNED TO THE GYM. WITHIN TWO MONTHS HE HAD LOST THE EXCESS WEIGHT, WAS ABLE TO GIVE UP THE MEDICATION HE WAS ON AND WAS A CHEERFUL, CONFIDENT MAN.

YOUR INSTANT SELF-WORTH UPGRADE

I am going to give you a guaranteed plan of action that I have used for myself and countless others. Follow these three steps and watch your self-worth soar.

STEP ONE – RESPECT YOURSELF

I want you to think hard about your religious and spiritual beliefs and practices. A religion that condemns you as being an unworthy sinner and requires you to spend the rest of your life atoning for your sins is not the ideal backdrop for feeling good about yourself as a human being. Even if you weren't brought up in a religious family the ideas that underpin many religions are very pervasive in our culture and tend to seep under your skin. I'm not urging you to give up all of your religion, but to question the parts of it that require you to see yourself as being intrinsically bad.

Many people are finding that organised religion no longer meets their needs and churches are experiencing one of the greatest crises of all time. In 1999, for example, a leading Irish training college for Catholic priests had no new students whatsoever. Two things are going on here: firstly, Christian religions are no longer providing satisfying answers to our spiritual and moral questions; secondly, we are experiencing the urge to come up with our own intensely personal answers, as part of the movement to take back responsibility for the core values that we hold. 'To thine own self be true' has never been more relevant.

It makes sense that Eastern religions are attracting increasing interest from the West. Both Hindu and Buddhist philosophies see human beings as intrinsically divine and do not share our Western belief in self-hatred.

The Dalai Lama was astonished when he first heard of self-hatred and its prevalence in Western culture, during a conference with scientists and psychologists at his home in Dharamsala in 1991. He said,

Although I'd thought I had some understanding of how the mind works, this idea of hating oneself was completely new to me . . . and quite unbelievable. From the Buddhist point of view being in a depressed state, in a state of discouragement is seen as a kind of extreme which can clearly be seen as an obstacle to taking the steps necessary to accomplish one's goals. A state of self-hatred is even more extreme than simply being discouraged and this can be very, very dangerous. For those engaged in Buddhist practice the antidote to self-hatred would be to reflect on the fact that all beings, including oneself, have Buddha nature, the seed or potential for perfection and full enlightenment. So those who suffer from self-hatred should . . . concentrate more on the positive aspects of their existence such as appreciating the tremendous potential that lies within oneself as a human being. We are gifted human beings with this wonderful human intelligence and all human beings have the capacity to be very determined and to direct that strong sense of determination in whatever direction they would like to use it.

This is a much more uplifting, inspiring approach to life. With this approach you can get up off your knees and give up atoning, concentrating instead on bringing forth positive qualities such as tolerance, respect and kindness to yourself and others.

A brilliant motivational teacher I met some years ago, Sonda Ray, explained this perfectly when she drew the analogy between God and a cherry pie, cut into slices. Each one of us is a slice, that is, we are all part of God and have divinity within us.

Why not make an altar to yourself? Find a photograph of yourself when you were about four, looking sweet and innocent. Put it in a lovely frame and position it in a corner of your bedroom with fresh flowers, incense, a candle and a picture of an inspiring spiritual teacher like Jesus or Buddha. This is your way of reminding yourself to honour yourself. As a divine being, guided by straightforward moral principles, how can you not like yourself? Surely you deserve the best and you have a responsibility to honour yourself and take care of yourself in mind, body and spirit. Showing yourself disrespect through habits such as overeating, drinking excess alcohol or smoking makes no sense. Nor does allowing others to be disrespectful.

EXERCISE

Answer the following questions:

1) *What do I do or tolerate in my life that demeans my divineness?*
2) *What am I willing to do to reduce or eliminate this in my life?*
3) *Are there people from whom I need to move away in my life?*
4) *What would I need to do to set new standards of self-respect and respect from others?*
5) *If I really believed I was intrinsically good this would leave me feeling . . .*
6) *And the biggest difference in my life would be . . .*

With this information I now require you to make decisions and *take action*. What decisions are you willing to make in the light of the insights you now have about your own self-worth? Are you ready to make time for regular exercise or massage treatments? Do you need to set some boundaries at work or in your personal life? Life revolves around the decisions you make, so make some really good ones now. And take one action today to demonstrate your intent: find the photograph, book a massage, set some new standards in a relationship of friendship.

Repeat the following affirming thoughts to yourself: *I now choose to treat myself with complete respect. The more I honour and respect myself, the more others do too. I am an innocent, loving, loveable human being. I deserve the best.*

Show yourself some serious respect now and enjoy!

STEP TWO – BE GOOD

How do you know that you're good? Are you a big, generous, expansive human being? Only you know the answers. More and more people are finding good in themselves. Over the past few years there has been a huge increase in giving. Increasing numbers of successful people have left well-paid jobs to work for charities at home and abroad. More and more people are taking the decision to give time, energy and effort to others.

Can you list ten indications of your goodness and largeness of spirit right now? If you have problems coming up with ten easily, then you may need to give yourself more opportunities to demonstrate the qualities of tolerance, respect and kindness.

You don't have to give huge amounts of time to a charity. You can consciously carry out little acts of kindness on a daily basis that don't require much extra time, just extra thought. Look after the most vulnerable people you know: children and the elderly. You can inspire children with well-chosen words that could really make a difference. Listening with interest and concern to an elderly man or woman on a bus may just make a difference to their day. And if you do decide to volunteer some of your time the rewards will be priceless. You'll feel terrific about yourself, you'll see your problems with less intensity and become more relaxed about your own issues.

Giving selflessly in this way brings with it a unique feeling of having made a contribution in a way that paid work doesn't. So if you want to see yourself as a thoroughly decent human being, go right ahead and be one. Make a contribution, make a difference and make your life important. Being good requires active service.

It's not surprising that affluent, successful people give huge amounts of time and energy to charity projects. Think of Live Aid, Comic Relief, The Aids Crisis Trust or Net Aid. Think of individuals like Elton John, George Michael, Robbie Williams, Dave Stewart and Annie Lennox, all of whom give so much. Or Bono and Bob Geldof, who together spearheaded the enormously successful campaign to cancel third world debt. Or Diana, Princess of Wales, who found meaning in her life through the incredible work she did for others.

Sometimes if a client of mine is concerned about bringing more balance and fulfilment into their life I suggest that deeper meaning and satisfaction may be found through giving time and effort to others.

On the other hand, things can go too far. Denise came to me when she realised she had been giving so much to worthy causes that she was neglecting herself and her family. I asked her to stop her charity work for six months and make herself and her children her top priority. There's absolutely no point in burning yourself out.

EXERCISE

List five new actions you are willing to take to increase your goodness and then take them straightaway.

STEP THREE — WIPE THE SLATE CLEAN

Clean, shiny, pristine self-worth requires a clear conscience. Low-level guilt lives under your skin, pervades your whole being and eats away at your self-worth. If you see yourself as bad or feel guilty then you'll put a brake on feeling that you deserve great things. You, above anyone else, must have a high opinion of yourself if you are to have self-worth.

So take this opportunity to detox, have a personal spring clean and rid yourself of any dust and grime that may be lurking around. Clearing past misdeeds, wrongdoings and mistakes paves the way for greater clarity and optimism. You'll feel lighter, cleaner and ready to sparkle. So let's get the slate out and start wiping.

EXERCISE

Make a list of everything you have done in the past that you feel uncomfortable about. Then complete these statements:

1) *Three things I do not forgive myself for are . . .*
2) *Three things I punish myself for are . . .*

Now to the slate-wiping part. First: *Check your interpretation of events.* Are you feeling that you've done wrong when actually you haven't? Are you feeling guilty or bad for something that wasn't within your power to change? It may be that you simply need to see events from a different perspective, as Alison (see below) did. Perhaps you have actually been coping well with a difficult situation. If so then give yourself credit for your bravery and determination.

Second: *Make amends.* If you have decided that you were really in the wrong then do something about it. Apologise, make a phone call, send a bunch of flowers or write a letter, even if the person concerned is dead and you can't send it. And then let go of the guilt. By holding on to guilt you may think you're absolving yourself, but you're not. Guilt is a signal that something needs putting right, so getting stuck with the signal becomes sheer indulgence.

Third: *Do something practical.* If you've really caused damage then do something tangible to re-balance the scales. If you can't alter the original situation then make a contribution that is as relevant as possible. For instance, if you stole some money and can't repay it to the original person or organisation, then give an equal amount to a worthy cause. This is sometimes the only way to move on.

Finally, use these affirmations:

I am now ready to forgive myself for . . .
I no longer need to punish myself for/feel guilty about . . .
I forgive myself totally.

ALISON'S STORY
ALISON WANTED TO FIND A QUALITY RELATIONSHIP. SHE WAS A
GORGEOUS PERSON AND NO ONE COULD UNDERSTAND HOW SHE
COULD HAVE PROBLEMS IN THIS AREA. BUT WITHIN TEN MINUTES OF
TALKING WE GOT TO THE NUB OF THE ISSUE. ALISON HAD BEEN
DIVORCED EIGHTEEN MONTHS EARLIER AND HAD BEEN LEFT WITH
SUBSTANTIAL DEBTS. HER STRICT MORAL CODE LEFT HER FEELING
EXTREMELY BAD ABOUT THIS. IT WAS LIKE A BIG, BAD, HIDDEN
SECRET THAT SHE KEPT LOCKED AWAY AND SHE WAS WORKING
SEVEN DAYS A WEEK TO REPAY THE DEBT. LETTING A MAN INTO HER
LIFE MEANT THAT HE MIGHT DISCOVER HER SECRET. AND EVEN MORE
SIGNIFICANTLY, SHE DIDN'T FEEL THAT SHE DESERVED TO HAVE FUN.
THIS WOULD HAVE BEEN LETTING HERSELF OFF THE HOOK. I POINTED

OUT TO ALISON HOW HARD SHE WAS BEING ON HERSELF. SHE WAS PUNISHING HERSELF FOR SOMETHING SHE SAW AS TERRIBLE AND THE RESULT WAS THAT SHE WAS PHYSICALLY DRAINED AND TENSE ALL THE TIME. I INVITED HER TO ADOPT A FAR MORE ACCURATE AND USEFUL INTERPRETATION OF HER SITUATION. IT WENT LIKE THIS: SHE WAS AN INCREDIBLY COURAGEOUS PERSON WHO HAD CHOSEN TO TAKE ON THE DEBT, WHICH SHOWED GREAT FAITH IN HERSELF. IT WAS A TRULY UPRIGHT THING TO DO. IT WOULD HAVE BEEN ALL TOO EASY TO DECLARE HERSELF BANKRUPT AND TO WALK AWAY, AS MANY PEOPLE DO. IN HER NEW INTERPRETATION SHE HAD EVERY RIGHT TO FEEL PROUD AND TO THINK OF HERSELF AS BRAVE AND RESOURCEFUL.

ALISON IMMEDIATELY SAW THAT I WAS RIGHT AND REALISED WHAT SHE HAD PUT HERSELF THROUGH. IT WASN'T THE SITUATION BUT HER INTERPRETATION OF IT THAT HAD CREATED HER TURMOIL. AFTER THIS ALISON BEGAN TO LIVE AGAIN. SHE CUT DOWN ON HER OVERTIME, LET FRIENDS KNOW SHE WAS AVAILABLE FOR DINNER PARTIES AND CHANGED THE MESSAGE SHE WAS SENDING OUT TO MEN FROM 'DO NOT DISTURB' TO 'I'M UP FOR FUN'.

YOUR REWARDS

Well Done! You've come a long way and you're still with me. Put a smile on your face and pat yourself on the back for staying the course so far. Your prize for all your application, suspension of disbelief and willingness to challenge yourself is the gift of glowing self-confidence and an increasingly magnetic personality.

Let me explain. By now, through playing your part, doing the exercises and taking action, you've worked to dig deep, excavate the debris and establish a solid foundation. Your self-image will be more defined and in place, and your self-worth hugely strengthened.

Now I'm going to show you the five simple steps towards

building powerful self-confidence on these foundations. Self-confidence will come easily to you after the work you've done so far. It rests lightly on the secure base of a great self-image and magnificent self-worth. And when you glow with confidence, as you will begin to do, then you become instantly more attractive and magnetic to others. You've already shown that you can make a real difference to the way you feel about yourself, and that difference will be reflected back to you by people and events around you.

THE FIVE STEPS TO GLOWING SELF-CONFIDENCE

STEP ONE – LIKE YOURSELF

The most important single ingredient of self-confidence is liking yourself. People who like themselves are light-hearted and optimistic; they are comfortable with themselves and easy to be around; they always seem to be lucky; and they are generous. Do you like you? Do you feel enthusiastic about who you are? Are you thankful for the particular qualities and talents that you have? Are you genuinely grateful to be you? If this is how you're feeling about yourself, then great. If not then complete the following exercise:

EXERCISE

Take pen and paper and write the answers to these statements:

1) *Ten things I like about myself right now are . . .*
2) *Five things that really mark me out as unique are . . .*
3) *Three things I've failed to notice or appreciate about myself are . . .*
4) *Three things about myself I wouldn't want to change are . . .*
5) *The main reason I'm glad I'm me is . . .*

Don't worry if finding enough answers is a bit of a challenge. You're beginning a habit that will stand you in good stead for the rest of your life – the habit of appreciating yourself. Keep practising and it will soon become automatic and feel quite natural.

STEP TWO – CHOOSE YOUR THOUGHTS CAREFULLY

You are the sum total of your thoughts. 'As a man thinketh so he is.' The only difference between an optimist and a pessimist is what they choose to focus on. It is often said that we have 90,000 thoughts a day and of these 60,000 are repetitive. In other words we think the same thoughts over and over again.

At any time you are free to choose which thoughts you hold on to and which ones you let go. I find that the majority of my new clients take their fearful, negative thoughts far more seriously than the optimistic, exciting ones. The excuse they come up with for this self-torture is that they're being 'realistic'. To break this habit you need to change direction, guard against reckless thoughts that will damage you and choose thoughts that will support and encourage you.

Any time you feel down, dejected or pessimistic, change your train of thought immediately. It really is that simple. Just say *no* to the thoughts that have created your miserable feelings and choose new thoughts that will create a feeling of optimism and cheerfulness.

I've already talked about affirmations in the last chapter (see page 32). These positive statements are a powerful and effective way of changing your thinking. The right affirmation should leave you feeling uplifted and enthusiastic. Affirmations should always be in the present tense and be phrased as though they are already the case. For instance, if you want a new job your affirmation might be: 'I now have my ideal job'. Repeat your affirmations as often as you can – certainly many times a day – so that thinking in these positive ways becomes a habit.

STEP THREE – STUDY CONFIDENT PEOPLE

A great way to achieve what you want in life is to find out how others have achieved it and then do the same things. Look out for people who have glowing self-confidence and notice their characteristics. Listen to the way they talk and look at the way they behave. There are two kinds of self-confident people. Those who have it innately and those who have taken the decision at some point to be self-confident and who have worked to achieve it.

Both types are fascinating. So seek them out, listen, learn and copy them. Notice the things they do that make an impact and try them yourself.

STEP FOUR – CHOOSE YOUR INFLUENCES

You can't avoid being exposed to all kinds of outside influences and opinions. These may include friends, family, newspapers, television programmes, politicians, religious leaders and many other sources of opinions and information. The news that is selected for us can paint a picture of a world that is relentlessly bleak. A couple of years ago British newsreader Martyn Lewis pointed this out and argued for a more balanced selection of news on television.

The important thing here is to be aware of what influences you and to make choices about the influences you choose. Flood your mind with the most inspiring and uplifting thoughts and ideas you can find. Read biographies of people who have done exceptional things, listen to inspiring tapes and begin to cut down and filter out the negative and pessimistic views that you encounter. Develop an immunity to pessimism so that you don't absorb it, and make sure that you spend at least thirty minutes each day reading or listening to something uplifting.

STEP FIVE – BEWARE COMPARISONS

The quickest way to deflate your well-earned self-confidence is to compare yourself to the wrong people. In a nanosecond you can puncture your pride in yourself, which is a terrible waste of time and means you'll have to work to re-build it. Don't put other people on pedestals. You may think someone else has a perfect life, but chances are that you actually know very little about that person or whether they are truly happy. And comparing yourself negatively to them is simply a way of trampling all over yourself.

If you want to compare yourself to anyone choose a comparison that will leave you feeling happy and grateful to be you. Remind yourself that there are many people who would be glad to change places with you and many more who think you're lucky and successful.

Even better, forget comparisons and instead choose great role models to follow – people who have qualities and characteristics that you really admire and from which you can learn.

JULIAN'S STORY
LET ME TELL YOU ABOUT JULIAN, A CLIENT OF MINE WHO WAS TERRIFICALLY COMMITED, WORKED HARD AND GOT GREAT RESULTS. ONE DAY HE SOUNDED TOTALLY DEJECTED, HIS USUAL CONFIDENCE AND *JOIE DE VIVRE* UTTERLY DEFLATED. HE TOLD ME HE FELT FED UP, LETHARGIC AND UNHAPPY WITH HIS LIFE AND HIS ACHIEVEMENTS. AFTER LISTENING TO THIS MY GUT FEELING WAS THAT HE'D DONE A GREAT JOB OF RUBBISHING HIMSELF BY COMPARING HIMSELF TO SOMEONE ELSE. WHEN I ASKED HIM ABOUT THIS HE AGREED THAT HE'D BEEN COMPARING HIMSELF TO A FAMOUS BILLIONAIRE WHO WAS ENORMOUSLY POWERFUL AND ABLE TO INFLUENCE THE ECONOMY OF AN ENTIRE COUNTRY.

WE BOTH LAUGHED, BUT NONTHELESS JULIAN HAD ALLOWED HIS

MIND TO RUN RIOT, TORTURING HIMSELF WITH RIDICULE AND ACCUSATION. ONCE HE REALISED WHAT HE WAS DOING HE STOPPED. TO PREVENT HIM DOING IT AGAIN I TOOK HIM THROUGH THIS PROCEDURE, WHICH YOU CAN USE WHEN YOU FEEL AN UNDERMINING SESSION COMING ON.

FIRST I QUESTIONED THE CHOICE OF THIS PARTICULAR BILLIONAIRE AS A COMPARISON. I ASKED JULIAN IF HE KNEW WHETHER THE BILLIONAIRE HAD A HAPPY FAMILY LIFE, SPENT TIME WITH HIS CHILDREN, HAD ANY TRUE FRIENDS, TOOK GOOD CARE OF HIS BODY AND ENJOYED VIBRANT GOOD HEALTH. ALL OF THESE THINGS WERE GREAT ACHIEVEMENTS FOR JULIAN, YET HE'D DISCOUNTED THEM IN HIS RUSH TO COMPARE HIMSELF. NEXT I ASKED JULIAN TO CHOOSE A DIFFERENT COMPARISON WITH SOMEONE ELSE, ONE THAT WOULD LEAVE HIM FEELING HAPPY AND GRATEFUL. AS SOON AS HE DID THIS JULIAN WAS ABLE TO APPRECIATE HIS ACHIEVEMENTS AGAIN. HE HAD SPENT DAYS WITH THE BILLIONAIRE'S SPECTRE LURKING IN THE SHADOWS, YET IT TOOK TEN MINUTES TO TURN HIS MOOD, ENERGY LEVELS AND OUTLOOK AROUND.

If you find you are comparing yourself poorly to someone else, stop it immediately. If there is a quality in the other person that you would like for yourself then by all means bring it into your life. But on no account must you use someone else's example to trample all over yourself. It may also be appropriate to shock yourself by introducing a whole new perspective. Remind yourself that there are people who would give anything to change places with you and to have your concerns and dilemmas. Its important to remember that we are very lucky to be here, with all our concerns, and not in Bosnia or another war torn country, or in any of the other places where people are suffering terribly. Every five seconds someone dies of hunger. Two-thirds of the world will die without ever having used a computer. Pull yourself up sharp, jolt yourself into a fresh perspective any time you need to and remind yourself of how lucky you actually are.

YOUR MAGNETIC PERSONALITY

Someone with a magnetic personality attracts into their lives favourable people and circumstances. So how do you create a magnetic personality? Simply by building your foundations of self-image, self-worth and glowing self-confidence and having high-quality thoughts about yourself.

You have attracted everything in your life. So why not make sure that you attract only the best: the most loving, reliable, supportive people, the most favourable circumstances, the great pieces of luck and plenty of success. Pessimism and optimism, lightness and heaviness, cheerfulness and misery are all highly contagious and all carry their own energy. As you are now committed to entertaining only the very best, highest-quality, most optimistic thoughts then you will now begin to attract people who are drawn to this uplifting energy of yours and who have similar qualities.

Because you like yourself more now and are comfortable with yourself you are much more fun and easy to be around. You are more relaxed, less intense and worried and more spontaneous. You are developing a magnetic personality.

YOUR ASSIGNMENT

Now I want you to give yourself a reward. Your assignment is to take yourself out to dinner! Seriously. I request that you treat yourself to something that smacks of a special treat for you. If dinner isn't your ideal treat then choose something else. Here are some suggestions, choose one and then *take action*:

- Take yourself out to lunch or breakfast or simply to enjoy a great cup of coffee in a café. Toast yourself.
- Pamper yourself with a luxurious bathtime experience. Imagine that you are preparing this treat for a very special person. Arrange scented candles, play soft music, burn essential oils or incense, pour a glass of wine and fill the bath with bubbles. Then lie back and repeat *I like myself* ten times.
- Cook yourself a terrific, nutritious meal.
- Take yourself to the cinema or theatre.
- Buy yourself a great novel and take time out to read it.
- Do something you've always wanted to try – horse-riding, ice-skating, trampolining, a yoga class or singing lessons.
- Or simply use your imagination and come up with a great idea of your own.

Enjoy!

AND REMEMBER . . .

Indestructible self-belief brings serenity, security and self-acceptance.
    Everything in your life is a reflection of what you feel you deserve.
    Learn to love yourself and you'll never need anyone else's approval again.
    Appreciate yourself for all that you do and are.
    Be more generous to others, and especially the more vulnerable among us.

CHAPTER FOUR

Cultivate Self-reliance, Personal Power and Irresistible Charisma

T HE NEXT building block you are going to put in place as you become someone who lives the life you really want is the ability to rely absolutely and totally on yourself. You already have the strong foundation of a high-quality self-image and secure self-worth. With these two characteristics in place you can now construct a new and exciting level of self-reliance.

Self-reliance is the most useful attribute that you can develop. With powerful and healthy levels of self-reliance you will never again look to others to sort, fix, mend or organise your life for you. You will understand that you alone are responsible for the life you have and that you alone are able to create it. True self-reliance will leave you glowing with confidence and make you hugely attractive to others.

Self-reliance is like a muscle. You can use it or lose it. If you haven't practised self-reliance on a regular basis then it will be flabby from lack of exertion. But, flex and stretch it enough and it will grow bigger, stronger and tough enough to cope with whatever demands you place upon it. Self-reliance is the single universal quality that truly powerful individuals share. It is what separates high achievers from their followers, imitators and critics. It intrigues and attracts others to them and gives them personal poise and irresistible charisma.

People who are self-reliant stand out because they have learned to look inside themselves for answers and solutions. In doing so they have developed a happy and healthy relationship with themselves.

In his book *The Road Less Travelled* M. Scott Peck says: 'Most of us believe that the freedom and power of adulthood is our due, but we have little taste for adult responsibility and self-discipline.' Developing self-reliance is about developing these qualities of responsibility and self-discipline and, in a true – and truly exciting – sense, becoming an adult.

TRUE POWER

Those who are completely self-reliant have real power. What is normally considered to be power is not real power at all. Chasing money, glamour or sex, wanting control over others, and political and military power are simply manifestations of the need to appear powerful. A person can be in a position of power and influence and still be very weak, without a shred of real personal power and internal ease. Heads of government, heads of major companies, television personalities, film stars and people at the very pinnacle of their professions may not have it and money definitely can't buy it. I have certainly worked with people who have a great deal of authority and who wield great power externally. Oftentimes they are internally indecisive and weak.

You can be rich, successful and neurotic. In fact, money can make you more neurotic, if you rely on it as the source of your power, because you'll live on a knife edge, with the fear that it could all be taken away from you.

Trying to win people over, seeking approval and acceptance, trying to impress and craving praise all create weakness and destroy your real power, because they make you dependent on other people's whims. You end up being a puppet controlled by others' moods and choices.

Self-importance is very different to self-worth. Self-importance is what insecure people hide behind, in an attempt to convince others that they matter. Writer Carlos Castaneda put it perfectly when he said: 'Most of our energy goes into upholding our importance. If we were capable of losing some of that importance two extraordinary things would happen to us. One, we would free our energy from trying to maintain the illusory idea of our grandeur and two, we would provide ourselves with enough energy to catch a glimpse of the actual grandeur of the universe.'

Real power comes from self-reliance, and those who have this strong internal power stand out from others. It gives them freedom to speak their minds and live as they please. Their self-approval allows them to sail through life without excessive turmoil and angst. Think Nelson Mandela, Anita Roddick, the late Linda McCartney and Sir Paul McCartney, Oprah Winfrey, Margaret Thatcher, Tony Benn, Gandhi, Martin Luther King, Emily Pankhurst, the Dalai Lama, Winston Churchill and Germaine Greer. Look at Hilary Clinton, Cherie Blair, Vivienne Westwood, Tina Turner, Donatella Versace, Vanessa Redgrave and Bette Davis.

Many others have been portrayed in films. Think of Liam Neeson in *Michael Collins,* Brad Pitt in *Seven Years in Tibet,* Mel Gibson in *Braveheart,* Daniel Day Lewis in the *Last of the Mohicans,* Sigourney Weaver in *Gorillas in the Mist,* Tim Robbins in *Shaw-*

shank Redemption, Denzel Washington in *The Hurricane* and Vivien Leigh in *Gone with the Wind*. All these people and characters ooze self-approval, self-reliance and personal power. They are effortlessly charismatic. They just shine. You don't have to like them or agree with them to see that they have integrity, poise and a devil-may-care attitude.

Margaret Thatcher was loved and loathed with equal passion, but even her critics admired her willingness to shoot from the hip, not giving a darn what anyone thought of her. She didn't canvass public opinion before she voiced an opinion.

On the other end of the political spectrum, veteran left-winger Tony Benn is the same. He speaks his mind and he stands out a mile from others in this respect. Even those who don't share his opinions admire his gutsiness. Germaine Greer, a pioneer of the women's liberation movement, is a controversial, free, exciting, unpredictable and original thinker. Another is writer Julie Burchill. She was the most highly paid and talked-about columnist in the UK because she said exactly what she thought, no matter how outrageous.

You can spot true internal power because the people who have it also have enormous charisma. The more self-reliance you develop, the more real power you will generate for yourself. And that will make you immensely attractive to other people.

Before I go on to explain the steps involved in developing this kind of internal power and self-reliance, let me tell you the stories of two fascinating and very different people, Emma and Paul.

EMMA'S STORY
EMMA HAD BEEN WORKING AS A DEPUTY EDITOR ON A NATIONAL NEWSPAPER FOR SEVEN YEARS, REGULARLY WORKING THROUGH THE NIGHT FOR UP TO FIVE NIGHTS A WEEK. HER JOB WAS HUGELY

DEMANDING AND STRESSFUL, THE PACE RELENTLESS, THE WORKING ATMOSPHERE HOSTILE AND PANIC-STRICKEN AND THE STAFF COMPETITIVE AND INSECURE, TERRIFIED OF LOSING THEIR JOBS.

SURVIVING IN THIS EDGY, NEUROTIC ENVIRONMENT HAD TAKEN ITS TOLL ON EMMA'S HEALTH AND LIFESTYLE. SHE HAD LOST CONTACT WITH FRIENDS, SHE FELT ILL AND UNFIT, EXTRA WEIGHT HAD PILED ON AND SHE HAD GIVEN UP GOING TO THE GYM BECAUSE SHE WAS ALWAYS SO TIRED. EMMA WAS THIRTY-FIVE BUT LOOKED A WORN-OUT FORTY-FIVE AND SHE HAD FINALLY REACHED THE POINT WHERE SHE COULD STAND IT NO LONGER. EMMA RESIGNED, DETERMINED NEVER TO LIVE LIKE THAT AGAIN. AFTER A HOLIDAY AND A FEW WEEKS' REST SHE CONTACTED ME TO HELP HER PLAN THE NEXT STAGE OF HER LIFE.

AT THIS POINT EMMA HAD NO CLEAR IDEA OF WHAT SHE WANTED TO DO. SHE HAD MANAGED TO SAVE QUITE A BIT, MAINLY BECAUSE HER LONG WORKING HOURS MEANT SHE NEVER HAD TIME TO SHOP OR GO OUT! SHE HAD A NICE FLAT IN CENTRAL LONDON, BUT PAYING FOR IT WAS EATING INTO HER SAVINGS AND EMMA WAS ANXIOUS TO GET HER LIFE GOING AGAIN.

I FOUND EMMA DEEPLY UNHAPPY AND CONFUSED, WITH LITTLE APPRECIATION OF THE TREMENDOUS TALENTS SHE OBVIOUSLY HAD AND THE UNLIMITED OPPORTUNITIES AVAILABLE TO HER. EMMA WAS TRYING TO FIND THE ANSWER TO WHAT SHE SHOULD DO WITH HER LIFE BY ASKING FRIENDS, FORMER COLLEAGUES, FAMILY AND JUST ABOUT EVERYONE SHE KNEW — EXCEPT HERSELF. SHE THOUGHT AN INTERNET BUSINESS MIGHT BE A GOOD IDEA, AS THAT WAS SOMETHING EVERYONE ELSE SEEMED TO BE DOING, BUT IT WASN'T SOMETHING SHE FELT STRONGLY ABOUT. EMMA WAS GETTING INCREASINGLY ANXIOUS, AND HER FAMILY PILED ON THE PRESSURE BY PHONING HER ALL THE TIME WITH MORE IDEAS ABOUT WHAT SHE COULD DO.

My first step was to forbid Emma to ask for ideas, suggestions and advice from everyone around her. I appreciated that her friends and family were being caring and trying to help, but their involvement was actually stopping Emma from thinking clearly and trusting herself. Once Emma had agreed to this I asked her to go and find a job. That very day! Emma had been feeling listless, lethargic and dispirited for about six weeks. The benefits of her holiday and rest were long over. She was a dynamic, capable young woman who needed to be out in the world, mixing with people, enjoying herself and earning money.

'What sort of job did you have in mind?' Emma asked me, incredulously.

'How about waiting on tables in a trendy, stylish, fun restaurant?' I suggested.

Emma loved this idea, but came up with umpteen reasons why she couldn't do it. She was too old, overweight, not trendy enough and not pretty enough. And when we had worked through these objections we got to the real stumbling block. The most stylish restaurants were all frequented by her former colleagues and bosses. What would they think of her, waiting on tables? Wouldn't they think she was desperate, had fallen on hard times, should never have left the paper?

I pointed out the truth of the situation, which was that she was actually thrilled at the thought of working in one of these hip places and hanging out with fun, young people. What was stopping her was the thought of what other people might think of her. In other words, someone else's opinion — her former boss's for instance — was dictating her decisions and the course of her life. Emma was utterly

TRAPPED, A PRISONER OF HER OWN MAKING. SHE HAD GIVEN ALL THE POWER TO SOMEONE ELSE — AND NOT EVEN SOMEONE WHO SHE LIKED OR RESPECTED OR WHO HAD HER BEST INTERESTS AT HEART.

ONCE I HAD LAID BARE THE FACTS EMMA WAS SHOCKED. NEXT I INVITED HER TO SEE THE WAITRESSING JOB IN A POSITIVE LIGHT. I SUGGESTED THAT HER FORMER COLLEAGUES MIGHT ACTUALLY BE DEEPLY IMPRESSED AT HER GUTS AND CONFIDENCE IN TAKING SUCH A DIFFERENT JOB. THEY WOULD SEE THAT SHE WAS TAKING TIME OUT, MAKING MONEY AND HAVING SOME FUN BEFORE THE NEXT 'SERIOUS' STAGE OF HER LIFE. SOME WOULD SECRETLY WISH THEY HAD THE COURAGE AND INNER STRENGTH TO BREAK OUT AND CHANGE THE DIRECTION OF THEIR LIVES. ARMED WITH THIS NEW PERSPECTIVE EMMA AGREED TO PUT ON BRIGHT RED LIPSTICK, LOOK GREAT AND GO OUT AND GET A JOB.

WE SPOKE FOUR DAYS LATER AND EMMA HAD GOT NOT ONE BUT TWO JOBS, AT PRECISELY THE KIND OF FUN, STYLISH PLACES UPON WHICH WE HAD AGREED. SHE HAD ALREADY DONE A SHIFT IN ONE OF THEM AND, ALTHOUGH SHE WAS EXHAUSTED, SHE WAS LOVING IT. SHE COULD SEE THAT SHE WAS COMING TO LIFE AGAIN BY JUST BEING OUT IN THE WORLD OF WORK, MIXING WITH OTHER PEOPLE AND MAKING MONEY. THREE WEEKS LATER EMMA WAS STILL DOING BOTH JOBS; SHE'D LOST SOME WEIGHT EFFORTLESSLY, HAD A FABULOUS NEW HAIRSTYLE, LOOKED YEARS YOUNGER AND HAD REGAINED HER OLD CHEERFULNESS AND BRIGHTNESS.

EMMA HAD COME THROUGH HER CRISIS AND NOW SHE WAS IN THIS NEW, UPBEAT FRAME OF MIND WE COULD BEGIN TO IDENTIFY THE WAY FORWARD. WE NEEDED TO FIND OUT WHAT EMMA'S TRUE PASSIONS WERE, WHAT SHE WAS GOOD AT AND WHAT SHE SECRETLY DESIRED. SHE HAD LISTENED TO SO MANY PEOPLE'S ADVICE THAT SHE HAD NO IDEA WHAT SHE REALLY WANTED. SO I ASKED HER TO MAKE A LONG LIST OF THE THINGS SHE REALLY ENJOYED DOING AND NOT TO

THINK ABOUT WHETHER THEY COULD MAKE A SUCCESSFUL LIVING FOR HER OR NOT. WE SCALED HER INITIAL LIST DOWN TO THREE THINGS: WRITING, ORGANISING DINNER PARTIES AND SOCIAL GATHERINGS AND WATCHING FORMULA ONE RACING DRIVING. ALTHOUGH EMMA HAD BEEN AN EDITOR ON THE PAPER SHE HADN'T ACTUALLY DONE A LOT OF WRITING AND SHE'D ALWAYS ENVIED THE WRITERS WHO DID THE REALLY MEATY FEATURES AND INTERVIEWS. AND HER PASSION FOR FORMULA ONE HAD BEGUN WHEN SHE WAS INTRODUCED TO IT BY HER BROTHER'S FRIEND AT THE AGE OF FOURTEEN. EMMA HAD BEEN CAPTIVATED AND SINCE THEN HER DREAM HAD BEEN TO BE INVOLVED IN THIS WORLD IN SOME WAY.

WE EXPLORED HOW THESE THREE PASSIONS COULD LEAD TO A VARIETY OF BUSINESSES AND CAREERS. WHAT EMMA NEEDED ABOVE ALL WAS TO CONQUER HER NERVES, MAKE SOME DECISIONS AND TAKE ACTION. SHE HAD GOT INTO THE HABIT OF ALLOWING HER FEAR AND ANXIETY TO HOLD HER BACK AND TO RENDER HER IMMOBILE. SO THE MOTTO I GAVE HER TO LIVE WITH FOR THE WEEKS TO COME WAS: *CARRY ON REGARDLESS.* I URGED HER TO OVERCOME HER FEARS BY SIMPLY OVERRIDING THEM AND IGNORING THEM. SHE WAS TO CARRY ON WITH HER AGREED PLAN OF ACTION REGARDLESS OF HOW SHE WAS FEELING. IT WORKED PERFECTLY. TWO MONTHS LATER EMMA WAS WORKING FULL-TIME AS A WRITER, REGULARLY WRITING ABOUT FORMULA ONE RACING, AND WAS LOOKING AND FEELING TERRIFIC.

THE MOST IMPORTANT DECISION EMMA TOOK WAS TO STOP LISTENING TO OTHER PEOPLE AND TO START LISTENING TO HERSELF. THE SECOND MOST IMPORTANT DECISION SHE MADE WAS TO STOP PAYING ATTENTION TO HER FEARS. IN MAKING THESE TWO DECISIONS SHE WAS TOUGHENING UP AND DEVELOPING PSYCHOLOGICAL MUSCLE AND THE STAMINA, FLEXIBILITY AND SELF-AWARENESS NEEDED FOR TRUE SELF-RELIANCE.

PAUL'S STORY

I MET PAUL AND HIS WIFE ON HOLIDAY. CHATTING OVER BREAKFAST AT OUR HOTEL I WAS STRUCK BY THE WAY PAUL OOZED SELF-RELIANCE FROM EVERY PORE. HE HAD BEEN MADE REDUNDANT FROM HIS JOB AS A CONSTRUCTION TRAINER FOUR YEARS EARLIER, AT THE AGE OF THIRTY-TWO.

'ONCE THE SHOCK OF THE REDUNDANCY WORE OFF I BEGAN TO WONDER WHAT IT WOULD BE LIKE TO WORK FOR MYSELF. I THINK I'D ALWAYS SECRETLY WANTED TO TRY IT,' HE TOLD ME. 'THE REDUNDANCY WAS MY CHANCE TO MAKE THE BREAK. I ALSO SAW IT AS A CHANCE TO TRY A COMPLETE CHANGE AND MOVE SOMEWHERE COMPLETELY DIFFERENT.'

AFTER THAT EVERYTHING HAD HAPPENED VERY QUICKLY. PAUL AND HIS WIFE MARGARET SOLD THEIR HOUSE WITHIN DAYS OF PUTTING IT ON THE MARKET, PACKED UP THEIR CAR AND MOVED FROM NEWCASTLE, IN THE NORTH-EAST OF ENGLAND, TO GUILDFORD, IN THE SOUTH. THEY KNEW NO ONE AND STAYED IN CHEAP GUESTHOUSES UNTIL THEY FOUND A FLAT TO RENT. 'IT FELT LIKE AN ADVENTURE,' PAUL TOLD ME. 'WE WERE BOTH 100 PERCENT COMMITTED TO GOING IT ALONE AND SETTING UP A SUCCESSFUL BUSINESS. ONCE WE HAD MADE THE DECISION WE NEVER WAVERED. FAILURE JUST WASN'T AN OPTION.'

ONCE THEY HAD THEIR FLAT PAUL AND MARGARET SET ABOUT STARTING A CONSTRUCTION TRAINING COMPANY. AT THE OUTSET THEY BOTH SPENT THREE DAYS A WEEK SENDING OUT LETTERS TO POTENTIAL CUSTOMERS AND COLD CALLING OTHERS. IT WAS TO BE SIX MONTHS BEFORE THEY EARNED ANY MONEY. THEY LIVED MODESTLY AND BOTH TOOK PART-TIME JOBS, BUT THEY NEVER FALTERED IN THEIR RESOLVE TO MAKE IT WORK. SIX MONTHS AFTER STARTING OUT PAUL GOT HIS FIRST CONTRACT, IRONICALLY FROM THE COMPANY THAT HAD MADE HIM REDUNDANT IN THE FIRST

PLACE. THIS CONTRACT WAS RENEWED AND SLOWLY OTHER COMPANIES CAME ON BOARD AND WORD SPREAD THAT PAUL AND MARGARET'S WAS A GOOD BUSINESS.

PAUL'S SUCCESS DID NOT COME OVERNIGHT. BUT WHEN WE SPOKE HE HAD ENOUGH WORK COMING IN TO EMPLOY THREE OTHER CONSTRUCTION TRAINERS AND HE WAS EARNING FIVE TIMES THE SALARY HE HAD EARNED FOUR YEARS EARLIER. BUSINESS WAS COMING TO HIM EASILY AND HIS ONLY CONCERN WAS COPING WITH THE WORKLOAD AND FINDING THE RIGHT EMPLOYEES.

THE KEY TO HIS SUCCESS LAY IN SOMETHING MARGARET TOLD ME. 'WE COULDN'T FAIL,' SHE SAID. 'PAUL IS THE SORT OF PERSON WHO WOULD DO WHATEVER IT TOOK TO EARN THE RENT. HE WOULD HAVE GONE BACK TO HIS FIRST JOB, BRICKLAYING, IF HE'D HAD TO, UNTIL THE BUSINESS TOOK OFF.'

PAUL'S STRENGTH LAY IN HIS MENTAL APPROACH AND HIS WILLINGNESS TO TAKE ACTION AND KEEP ON TAKING ACTION UNTIL HE ACHIEVED HIS RESULTS. HIS MENTAL APPROACH WAS TWO-FOLD. FIRSTLY HE BELIEVED THAT FAILURE WAS NOT AN OPTION AND SECONDLY HE WAS ADAPTABLE ENOUGH TO DO OTHER THINGS, HOWEVER MENIAL, TO EARN MONEY IN THE SHORT TERM.

WHY SELF-RELIANCE IS VITAL

Emma and Paul were very different from one another, yet both showed a high degree of courage and determination. Emma was forced into developing self-reliance, while Paul had it innately, without even being aware of what he had. What Emma developed, through her own perseverance, and Paul had as an inbuilt gift, was a strong degree of internal resilience and a willingness to take action. And both of these qualities are needed to handle life today, when the demands are bigger and the pressures greater than ever before. There is no longer such a thing as job security or a job for life; these are memories from a bygone age. We are being encouraged to take responsibility for our own welfare and not to rely on the state or any outside agency. We cannot and must not wait to be rescued. There is a cultural, social and economic insistence that we all become self-sufficient entrepreneurs, endlessly flexible, imaginative and self-reliant. Never before has it been more important for all of us to become truly self-reliant.

People with a high degree of self-reliance have an air of authority, resilience and depth that separates them from those who shirk such individual responsibility. They have, in many cases, worked relentlessly to develop the courage and fearlessness which has taken them to great heights, in preference to the helplessness of relying on another human being or organisation to provide for their basic material, psychological, spiritual and emotional needs.

Such individuals will be direct, straightforward and without guile and will have the highest degree of integrity. Diana, Princess of Wales, was another woman who, like Emma, had learned self-reliance. In the last year of her life she had made peace with herself, conquered her eating disorder and forged a new relationship with herself, based on self-respect. As a result she was able to enjoy her own company, rely on her own judgement and make decisions for which she knew she would be heavily criticised. Her personal decision to head the Red Cross campaign against landmines brought condemnation from the Conservative government at the time. But because she had decided to trust her own judgement she was able to make decisions on this basis, without being swayed by the political or public response. And of course the political response was, eventually, to follow Diana's lead and accept that she had made the right decision. As she changed and grew Diana became more charismatic than ever and was growing into a globally influential human being.

BE ONE OF THE WINNERS

If you want to feel powerful, glow with charisma and exude poise you have to earn it. You have to reach down to your inner resources of strength and courage, build trust and respect for yourself and then demonstrate this to yourself by taking action.

People with invincible self-reliance have a secret, a knowing that marks them out as different. And that's simply because they have looked within when others would have floundered by looking outside themselves for reassurance and guidance. They know they can rely on themselves because they have tested themselves and passed with flying colours. They've earned their badge of honour and they wear it with pride. What could be better than being taken seriously? To have the confidence not to care about whether people take you seriously or not but instead to live with your own respect and approval? What could be better than other people's love and admiration? Better still, how great is it to have your own self-love and self-acceptance? As French writer and philosopher Montaigne said; 'The greatest thing in the world is to know how to be oneself.'

And, I might add, how to love oneself.

EXERCISE

Take pen and paper and answer these questions:

1) *How much do I show faith in myself?*
2) *When was the last time I made a major decision using my own judgement?*
3) *How much do I need other people's approval?*
4) *How much do I like, respect and approve of myself?*
5) *When was the last time I took a risk that demonstrated faith and trust in myself, regardless of what others thought?*
6) *What would my life look like if I backed myself 100 percent, trusted myself and didn't look for respect and approval from others?*

THE SELF-RELIANCE MASTERPLAN

Self-reliance is the key that will open up a world of fearlessness, freedom and opportunity. Increasing your self-reliance to dizzying heights is not only possible, but it's achievable in a remarkably short space of time, if you are focused and determined enough. Here are the five steps to complete and utter self-reliance.

STEP ONE – BEFRIEND YOURSELF

Being your own best friend is the most powerful thing you can do for yourself. Imagine a best friend, or think of someone you actually know, who you not only like immensely, but respect enormously as well. You want the best for this person and you are totally on their side. You are rooting for them all the way and you are unquestionably, unequivocally loyal. Now please turn around, face yourself and have this same relationship with the person you see before you. Make the decision right now to commit to a meaningful relationship with yourself and to demonstrate fairness, loyalty, respect, tolerance, forgiveness and compassion.

Sometimes I hear people say the most insulting things about themselves, without realising how much they are undermining and demoralising themselves. Speak to yourself always as you would to a treasured friend. Point out to yourself how well you are doing and begin to enjoy your own company and to recognise what an interesting, amusing and fun person you are to be with.

LINDY'S STORY
LINDY WAS 7KG (16LB) OVERWEIGHT AND LOATHED HERSELF. EVERY DAY SHE WOULD LOOK IN THE MIRROR AND CALL HERSELF AN 'UGLY BITCH'. IS THIS WHAT YOU WOULD SAY TO YOUR BEST FRIEND TO MOTIVATE THEM TO EAT MORE HEALTHILY, GO TO THE GYM AND FEEL BETTER ABOUT THEMSELVES? ABSOLUTELY NOT. AND DID THIS

CRITICISM GET LINDY ANYWHERE? OF COURSE NOT. IT SIMPLY KEPT HER STUCK IN A SPIRAL OF SELF–DISGUST, LETHARGY AND COMFORT EATING.

WHEN I MET LINDY SHE'D BEEN FEELING THIS WAY FOR SIX MONTHS. WHEN I ASKED HER WHY SHE INSULTED HERSELF SHE SAID THAT SHE FELT SHE DIDN'T DESERVE TO BE SPOKEN TO MORE NICELY UNTIL SHE HAD SUMMONED UP THE WILLPOWER TO GET HER BODY UNDER CONTROL AND LOSE WEIGHT. WHEN I POINTED OUT THAT HER STRATEGY HAD BEEN IN PLACE FOR OVER SIX MONTHS AND HAD PRODUCED ABSOLUTELY NO RESULTS SHE WAS GENUINELY SHOCKED. SHE HADN'T NOTICED THAT SHE HAD FAILED TO MAKE ONE IOTA OF PROGRESS; SHE HAD SIMPLY GONE ON BEING NASTY TO HERSELF IN THE HOPE THAT IT WOULD WORK.

I ASKED LINDY WHETHER SHE WOULD SPEAK TO AN HONOURED BEST FRIEND USING THIS KIND OF ABUSIVE LANGUAGE. SHE REACTED ANGRILY, SAYING THAT SHE WOULDN'T DREAM OF SPEAKING TO ANYONE ELSE LIKE THAT, LET ALONE SOMEONE SHE LIKED. THE MOMENT SHE SAID THIS SHE REALISED THAT SHE WAS BEHAVING LIKE AN ENEMY TO HERSELF BY BEING ABUSIVE, THREATENING, INSULTING AND UNDERMINING.

I ASKED LINDY TO EXPERIMENT BY LIVING FOR ONE WEEK AS HER OWN BEST FRIEND, OFFERING HERSELF MORAL SUPPORT, ENCOURAGING WORDS, KINDNESS AND CONSIDERATION. I ASKED HER TO DO AND SAY ALL THE THINGS SHE WOULD IF SHE WERE SUPPORTING A CLOSE FRIEND.

LINDY AGREED, AND AFTER A WEEK SHE REPORTED BACK THAT SHE HAD ABSOLUTELY LOVED TREATING HERSELF SO DIFFERENTLY. WHAT'S MORE, THE DIFFERENCE IT MADE TO HER MORALE AND ENERGY LEVELS WAS STAGGERING. HER NEED FOR COMFORT FOOD DWINDLED AS SHE GAVE HERSELF REAL COMFORT IN THE FORM OF KIND WORDS AND SUPPORT. SHE NEGOTIATED WITH HERSELF OVER

GOING TO THE GYM, REWARDING HER EFFORTS WITH A MASSAGE. AT THE END OF THE WEEK LINDY HAD LOST 2KG (5LB) AND WAS FEELING MUCH LIGHTER IN BODY AND IN SPIRIT. LINDY HAD DISCOVERED HOW MUCH EASIER LIFE COULD BE WITH HER OWN BACKING AND SHE WENT ON TO LOSE THE REST OF HER EXCESS WEIGHT EASILY AND COMFORTABLY.

STEP TWO – TALK LESS

Powerful people talk less. Powerful people don't waste words, waffle on about nothing in particular or drift from one piece of chat to another. They think about what they want to say and express those thoughts clearly and purposefully to the relevant people. They are discreetly comfortable with themselves; they don't need to sell themselves to anyone because they are already sold to themselves. They never argue, for there is no point to be scored, no position to defend. As the classic Chinese text The Tao says: 'Those who know do not speak, those who speak do not know.'

We all know at least one person whose internal security, composure and comfort makes them irresistible and intriguing. They are easy to spot because they stand out without trying to and their ease affects everyone around them. The most powerful way to speak is with brevity, with nothing to prove and no need to impress, dominate the conversation or hear yourself talk. Make a point of listening at least twice as much as you talk. When I say listen I mean listen totally, without thinking of your reply as the other person is talking. When you listen fully in this way the other person will feel supported in your presence. You can let go of any need to dominate, persuade or compete. You will feel deeply secure, simply through your ability to listen and be silent, and you will take on a powerful charisma in doing so.

Most people talk for talking's sake. They exaggerate, invent things, talk without knowing or understanding what they're talking about or go over and over the same thing. They waste huge amounts of energy defending their point of view and trying to persuade others to share it. Don't bother trying to impress people; don't talk unless you have something to say and then keep it simple. When you are truly comfortable with yourself you won't need to be accepted or appreciated by others because you accept and appreciate yourself.

STEP THREE − KEEP YOURSELF TO YOURSELF

Be very selective in the things you choose to discuss about yourself with others. Develop the discipline of keeping your own counsel and being discreet about your life. When you discuss everything with everyone around you you waste enormous amounts of energy and you expose yourself to all kinds of undermining comments, criticisms and judgements. These often come from well-meaning people who think they are giving you useful advice. If something is important to you and you expose it to a large number of people, or discuss it simply for the sake of discussing it, then you will almost certainly meet discouragement and doubtfulness from others which will make it harder to believe in yourself and to follow your own path. The braver and more adventurous your ideas, ambitions and plans, the more likely it is that others will tell you that you can't achieve it.

Instead of looking to others for support, look to yourself. Having a meaningful relationship with yourself means keeping a degree of silence and secrecy about your life. Don't expose your soul fully to anyone else. Your personal and deeply felt philosophy about life and the universe should remain just that: personal.

The old adage 'Don't cast your pearls before swine' sums it up perfectly. If a belief, an intention or a thought is precious to you then don't share it with everyone around you. Of course you need to talk to the relevant people, those who will help you further your dreams and ambitions or support you on your way. But get very clear about who they are.

Whatever you do don't spill yourself all over people. Keep what's heartfelt and important close to your chest. Live with dignity and preserve the mystery of who you are. Don't give yourself away.

STEP FOUR – CURB NEEDINESS

Having a discussion with a friend to mull over an idea can be great. Leaning on others sometimes or asking for help occasionally is fine. But make sure it stops there. If you flounder and flail all over people, expecting them to resolve things for you, make you feel better and make your decisions for you then you're in a disaster zone.

Curb neediness by fixing yourself. Talk to yourself, compose yourself, take responsibility for resolving your own inner turmoil. Stand tall for yourself and don't expect other people to do all the work. Every time you turn to yourself for guidance, support and answers you feed your own power and improve your self-reliance.

Building yourself up at the expense of others is tantamount to being a vampire. You'll drain your friends and leave them exhausted and if you go on doing this they'll want to avoid you. In any case, feeling better by these means is only ever a short-term fix with temporary effects. Every time you ask someone else to bandage you up and dress your wounds you throw away the chance to do it for yourself.

Neediness is a huge turn-off. Displays of insecurity make people feel uncomfortable. Romantically it's a disaster. As the American relationship expert Chuck Spezzano says: 'When you're needy, you're hungry and the other person feels like lunch.' No wonder they want to run.

In every situation in life, whether it's a business deal, a relationship or something you want, your power lies in letting go of any neediness. If you remind yourself that you don't need it – that you can survive without it and walk away if you have to – you will be powerful. Stay in control and exude stability. Be strong, be brave and handle your disquiet and you will know that you can rely on yourself.

Be a little sought-after and don't make yourself too available in both personal and professional matters. Don't chase people or make too many phone calls. Give others a chance to want you. If you need to, organise some distractions for yourself. Get busy, take up a hobby, go away for the weekend, visit friends or throw a party. The more you want someone or something the more important it is to pull back and act like a confident self-assured person who never needs to chase after anything. Stand back and give whatever you want space to come to you. Or, as one wise woman said: 'Don't accept a Saturday date after Wednesday'!

TOM'S STORY

TOM USED HIS STAFF AS A CONSTANT CRUTCH TO REASSURE HIMSELF. HE HAD RECENTLY JOINED A LARGE ACCOUNTANCY FIRM AND HAD BEEN PROMOTED RAPIDLY. HE WAS CONSIDERABLY YOUNGER THAN SOME OF HIS STAFF AND FELT DEEPLY INSECURE AND CONSTANTLY ANXIOUS THAT OTHER PEOPLE WERE CRITICISING HIM. EVERY TIME HE FELT PANIC ABOUT THIS HE WOULD CALL HIS PERSONAL ASSISTANT OR SENIOR COLLEAGUES AND TALK IT OVER WITH THEM, TO MAKE HIMSELF FEEL BETTER. I POINTED OUT TO TOM THAT THIS WAS A BIT LIKE BLEEDING ALL OVER PEOPLE. AND APART FROM THE FACT THAT HE WAS BEING DEEPLY UNPROFESSIONAL AND FUELLING

OFFICE GOSSIP, IT DID HIM NO GOOD ANYWAY. HIS RELIEF LASTED AS LONG AS IT TOOK FOR THE NEXT RUMOUR TO REACH HIS DESK.

I FORBADE TOM FROM PICKING UP THE PHONE THE NEXT TIME HE GOT IN A STATE. HOWEVER NEEDY OR DESPERATE HE FELT, HE HAD TO GO 'COLD TURKEY' AND RESIST REACHING FOR HIS FIX. NO MATTER HOW HAD HE FELT HE MUST FIND HIS OWN WAY THROUGH.

WE CAME UP WITH A RANGE OF OTHER OPTIONS HE COULD CHOOSE FROM. HE HAD TO LEARN TO TALK HIMSELF OUT OF HIS NEEDINESS AND TO TRAIN HIMSELF TO MAKE OTHER PEOPLE'S OPINION OF HIM LESS IMPORTANT THAN HIS OPINION OF HIMSELF. IT WAS TOUGH, BUT TOM BROKE THE HABIT OF RELYING ON OTHERS IN A WEEK AND LEARNED TO TRUST HIMSELF AND HIS OWN JUDGEMENT. AND THE MORE HE DID SO THE MORE HIS ANXIETY REDUCED AND FADED.

STEP FIVE – APPROVE OF YOURSELF

The most draining, tedious and morale-destroying conversation you can have with yourself or anyone else is the one that focuses on your perceived imperfections. Whether it's your weight, your receding hairline, your forgetfulness, the piece of work you just did or anything else it's deadly boring for you and anyone else unfortunate enough to be within earshot.

By having conversations like this you turn yourself into a weak, powerless person whose need for outside approval undermines any chance of a resourceful, respectful relationship with yourself. How much of your attention, thinking and conversation is taken up with examining your failures and shortcomings?

This kind of attitude comes from years of conditioning, mostly by cultural images of perfection in the media. From birth you have been bombarded by these images and messages, which change from decade to decade and from culture to culture. At the moment, for example, the fashion for women in the West is for full, thick lips. In India and Africa, it is the precise opposite. So you can't win! During the heyday of the women's movement in the seventies and early eighties, feminists went to fashion extremes to show they no longer needed men's approval to feel good about themselves. Women cut their hair, replaced stilletos with comfortable, flat shoes and replaced tights with skirts and loose trousers. The message was clear for all to see: 'We like and approve of ourselves and no longer dress for anyone else's approval.' This may have led to some extremes, with some women looking as though they'd just stepped off a building site! Nonetheless, it was undeniably brilliant and revolutionary to consciously challenge and subvert cultural conditioning in this way.

I know. I was one of the building site ones!

Your conditioning has been taking place for twenty, thirty, forty, fifty years or more, since the day you were born. You don't even have to make a special effort to expose yourself to it. On the Underground travelling to work, on television and in newspapers and magazines, the current images of perfection are everywhere. And the damage these images do can be enormous. This is clear when you see how men are now being targeted by lifestyle and grooming magazines and eating disorders among men are rising accordingly.

So give yourself a break. Stop reading the magazines, switch the television off and stop comparing yourself to rigid, airbrushed images. Think of it as a detox and a chance for your system to recover. Stop having Bridget Jones–and Ally McBeal–type conversations with yourself or anyone else. Ally is a wimp, a self-obsessed neurotic bore who craves approval. Bridget, the heroine of Helen Fielding's hugely successful novel, is equally pathetic. She meticulously records her calorie intake, cigarettes smoked and glasses of wine drunk. She waits by the phone for her current beau to phone. There isn't a shred of self-approval or gutsiness in this woman's body.

Sadly, lots of people live like this and characters like Ally McBeal and Bridget Jones aren't the figures of disdain and ridicule that they should be. We are endeared to them because they play out our own weaknesses. Don't live like this. Expect far more of yourself and live with a high degree of self-approval. Be like Ally McBeal's colleague Nelle, who is feisty, full of herself, light, fun and doesn't suffer fools gladly. Think Madonna, Muhammad Ali, Dorothy Parker, Amelia Earhart, Mae West, John Wayne, Jessica Mitford. Think Liam Neeson in *Schindler's List*, Kevin Costner in *Dances with Wolves*, Susan Sarandon in *Thelma and Louise*, Julia Roberts in *Erin Brockovich*, Meryl Streep in *Silkwood*, Joan Crawford in *Mildred Pierce*, Tom Cruise in *The Firm*, Robin Williams in *Dead Poets Society*, Scarlet O'Hara in *Gone with the Wind* and, of course, James Bond. I'm not saying that these people are perfect! Simply that they have a high degree of self-approval.

If you want approval, approve of yourself. Say to yourself often: *I now approve of myself completely*. Then add:*Especially in the presence of . . . (men/women/other people or the name of someone specific)*. Remember that if you treat yourself as special others will see you as being special. Their behaviour towards you will mirror your feelings about yourself. If you approve of yourself you will be loved and admired for your integrity and strength.

Make sure you're not the person who's desperate for approval and busily trying to earn brownie points. Be the kind of gutsy, ballsy person who doesn't need to sit on the fence or gauge public opinion before speaking up. Be someone who is dynamic, effective and likeable.

Remember that you are far stronger than you think you are. The more you rely on yourself the easier it will become. When you feel at your most uncertain you'll need to be bravest and to resist the impulse to ask someone else to make you feel better. Believe that you can do it for yourself and you will. No one knows better than you what you need. Be kind to yourself but be tough as well. Don't ask for or give advice. Instead look inside for the courage that is waiting there. As the great book of Chinese philosophy, the *Tao Te Ching* says: 'To understand others is to have knowledge. To understand oneself is to be illuminated. To conquer others needs strength. To conquer oneself is harder still.'

YOUR ASSIGNMENT

First I want you to spend some quality time with yourself. Enjoy your own company on at least two separate occasions in the next week. Relax with yourself, take yourself out to something fun or just read yourself a great book. Secondly I want you to spend a day practising the self-reliance masterplan (see page 77). Be your own best friend, talk less, curb your neediness and give yourself some serious approval.

Thirdly I want you to do something to prove to yourself that you can stand on your own two feet. Here are a few suggestions:

- Go out for an evening with friends who drink and drink water and soft drinks instead.
- Complain about something firmly and politely, without apologising.
- Start talking to someone you find attractive or interesting, without worrying about appearing lonely or desperate. You won't!

Only you can do it. Be bold, be brave and be brilliant!

AND REMEMBER . . .

Those who are completely self-reliant have true power.

With healthy self-reliance you will never again look to others to sort, fix or organise your life.

Self-reliance is like a muscle to be developed and strengthened.

Develop internal resilience and a willingness to take action.

Look inside yourself, not outside, for solutions, reassurance and guidance.

CHAPTER FIVE

You Are Always Right, So Choose What You Want To Be Right About

S O FAR I've dealt with your self-image, your self-worth, your personal power and your self-reliance, encouraging you to build and strengthen your psychological fitness so that you can feel brilliant and expect the very best from yourself.

Now it's time to look at the thoughts and expectations you have about life, because in order for this sparkling new you to create the life you want, you need to understand why your life is the way it is now. In this chapter I want to put your beliefs under the spotlight. The direction and quality of your life is the result of your beliefs. Your thoughts, expectations and actions are all based on your beliefs. So to get to the root of why things are the way they are for you, we have to reach in deep to the beliefs you use to shape your life.

Let me explain just how powerful beliefs can be. Beliefs have the potential to create or destroy. Wherever our beliefs come from – and that is usually a mixture of our childhood influences and authority figures and other social and personal influences as we go through life – we come to accept them as absolute truths. We defend them and live by them, no matter what that costs us.

In some tribal societies the people's belief in the power and authority of the Shaman is so strong that if he tells someone they will die, they do so.

In the 'civilised' world we tend to invest this belief in doctors and medical practitioners. When they give out a prognosis of life expectancy we believe them and the vast majority of patients die within a few weeks of the doctor's predicted date.

There are many inspiring examples of the power of beliefs. Research into concentration camp inmates suggests that those who survived had a belief system that gave them the strength to survive. They believed they would survive and they were able to make sense of their experiences. In Victor Frankl's book, *Man's Search for Meaning*, he talks of his potentially devastating experiences in a concentration camp. Frankl was an Austrian psychiatrist whose wife and parents were murdered by the Nazis. He suffered appallingly at their hands. Yet, he and others like him were able to find a positive way of looking at what had happened to them. They were able to find personal meaning and a way of seeing the world that gave their experiences in the camps value. He writes:

We who lived in concentration camps can remember the men who walked through the huts comforting others, giving away their last piece of bread. They may have been few in number but they offered sufficient proof that everything can be taken away from a man but one thing, the last of the human freedoms, to choose one's attitude in any given set of circumstances, to choose one's way. The way in which a man accepts his fate and all the suffering it entails, the way in which he takes up his cross gives him ample opportunity, even in the most difficult circumstances, to add a deeper meaning to his life.

What Frankl demonstrates so movingly is that we can't control the world or what life hands us, but we can control our reaction to it. He knew that if his suffering had no meaning he would not be able to bear it and he was able to create something positive from the worst imaginable experience. If he can do that then you and I can create something of value from anything life hands us. It is a matter of remembering that we always have a choice.

The Christian *bible* tells us that faith can move mountains. What we know for certain is that it can add years to your life. Studies have proved beyond doubt that prayer can hasten recovery, both in those who pray and those who are prayed for. Other studies have proved that prayer and strong religious faith are linked to a longer, healthier life. I've said already that I want you to choose your religion with care and make sure it's one that encourages you to grow and feel good about who you are. A religion which you feel is supportive and positive can be life-enhancing.

A study of 28,000 people, which appeared in *Demography* magazine, revealed that worshippers who attend a service at least once a week live seven years longer than those who don't. Among the black community the extra life expectancy increased by an astonishing fourteen years. These people share the belief that God protects them, and this encourages them to be more optimistic. These positive beliefs help them to live longer. Sylvia McAndrews is a fine example of the power of belief. After she was told that her breast cancer had spread to her bones and she had just three months to live she decided to make a pilgrimage to Lourdes in France, where believers are often cured. Sylvia recalls: 'I remember that on the last day I was lying on the floor of the grotto, crying. I put my whole trust in Our Lady. Then I felt a warm feeling in my spine and I heard a voice that said: "Don't worry child, you'll be alright".'

What happened next was to confound the medical profession.

Sylvia was healed, all trace of the cancer had gone. 'Some people might say I am completely crackers,' Sylvia admits, 'but I believe in faith and prayer.'

The power of the placebo effect demonstrates brilliantly the effect that beliefs can have. A surgeon in America offered ten patients an operation to relieve an arthritic knee. Only five were given the real surgery. The other five were merely sedated while he gave them minor stabs on their knees so that they'd believe they'd had the operation. Six months later both groups reported that their arthritic pain was much better.

This study raised so many questions that a similar study of 180 people is now being carried out. Many other studies around the world have proven the power of placebo medicines and treatments, which is being taken increasingly seriously by the medical establishment.

Negative beliefs are equally powerful. According to scientists at the renowned Mayo Clinic in Minnesota, pessimism is a risk factor in early death in much the same way as high cholesterol or obesity. Their research, which followed a group of 800 people for more than thirty years, found that regardless of age or sect the most pessimistic tended to die earlier than the optimistic people.

There are many examples of how our beliefs shape our lives and even how long we live. In the rest of this chapter we will begin to explore your beliefs, how they are shaping your life and how you can choose to replace those that don't help and benefit you. I believe you picked up this book because – deep down – you've decided that you will not settle for less than your capability. Therefore, you must now choose beliefs that will open up possibilities and opportunities for you. You deserve no less.

THE NEED TO BE RIGHT

Human beings all share a need to be right in order to make sense of the world and to feel in control of our lives. As we gather our beliefs we also gather evidence to support them. That way, whenever we need to defend our position on a particular issue, we can dip into our bag of evidence and come up with the proof we need.

But, in reality, there is very little in life that is absolutely right or wrong. Mostly we just adopt a belief and then stick to it. And we interpret life and the events around us in the light of our beliefs. For example, look at the way we view other people. In my experience we fall into two camps. One believes that people are basically decent and, given a chance, will do you a good turn. The other believes that people are selfish, only out for themselves and, given a chance, will rip you off. Which is true? Simply the one you decide is true.

When I mentioned to a journalist friend how moved I was by the huge contributions some celebrities make to good causes his immediate response was to sneer; 'Hah! I can tell you why they do it, it's just for the free publicity.'

James believes that people are only out for themselves and can support his view with plenty of examples. To my mind this is a grim view of people and one I studiously avoid. The evidence I look for and accumulate supports my belief that people are basically good and are happy to help you if they can. Which of us is right? We can both put up very strong cases for our position. James will unconsciously be looking for the evidence he needs every time he reads a newspaper, watches television or has a conversation. I am doing the same thing. This is because we get what we expect and look for in life. For example, I didn't notice pregnant women until I was pregnant, then suddenly they were everywhere. The point I am making is that once we have chosen our beliefs we make sure we are right about them and very little can sway us. So it makes sense to choose beliefs that really work for us and support us in having great lives.

You may not have consciously chosen any of the beliefs you now hold. In fact, you probably took most of them on board before you were old enough to understand the concept. But the truth is that you can choose to change any of them or add to them right now and from here on.

Fifteen years ago I chose to turn my entire belief system on its head. In those days I lived in a different world to the one I inhabit now: same planet; different world. The world I chose to be part of then was a grim place, with people dying from starvation every few seconds, a terrifying arms race that could annihilate us all at any moment and governments that were all cruel and heartless. To reinforce this perspective I read books that confirmed this philosophy, chose like-minded friends and argued aggressively with anyone who disagreed. I even covered the walls of my squat with newspaper reports of catastrophes, inequalities and suffering. I was one seriously miserable person. I conditioned myself to focus exclusively on all that was wrong in the world.

After two years of this intense mental training I was ill and depressed. My life was drained of any joy and pleasure and my entire system felt toxic – my perspective was literally poisoning me. Things came to a head with the Live Aid concert, that extraordinary event that focused the world's attention on the terrible suffering in Ethiopia. Most of the people with whom I had surrounded myself viewed it with deep cynicism and sneered at the celebrities involved and at everyone who gave money.

At this point I realised I had to save myself. I was totally exhausted, had all the symptoms of ME and spent increasing amounts of time sleeping. I had reached the point where I no longer cared whether my beliefs were right or wrong. I just knew that they were destroying me and I had to find some new ones that would let me feel enthusiastic and optimistic about life again.

It took me at least eighteen months to create my new mind set, during which time I attended every motivational 'Get a Life' type course I could find, read all the books and listened to all the tapes.

Within a few months I felt good about life again, my energy had returned and I was able to begin creating the life I really wanted – a life full of excitement, energy and success.

EXERCISE

Start to notice the beliefs of those around you. Listen as people reveal their beliefs and then provide the evidence to support them. If they don't immediately come up with the evidence then ask a few subtle questions and you'll soon get it.

Notice which beliefs are limiting and pessimistic and which are optimistic and expansive.

WHAT ARE YOUR BELIEFS?

Now it's time to get clear about your own beliefs. You will have thousands of beliefs, but a few major ones will be shaping the world you have created for yourself. Which beliefs do you use to guide you? On which beliefs do you base your decisions? Which of your beliefs are propelling you forward and which are holding you back?

EXERCISE

Have some fun with this one. Take ten minutes to brainstorm all the beliefs you have about everything. Write down every belief you can think of, no matter how big or small.

Now make two separate lists, one for empowering beliefs and one for disempowering beliefs.

The empowering ones are the ones that fuel your life, the ones that galvanise you and make things possible. The disempowering ones curtail and restrict you.

Here are some examples of disempowering beliefs:

- *Life is a struggle.*
- *If you want something you've got to fight for it.*
- *People are only out for themselves.*
- *Once you hit forty it's downhill all the way.*
- *Nothing is for free.*
- *You get rich by being mean.*

Here are some examples of empowering beliefs:

- *People are basically good at heart.*
- *I'm the sort of person who always finds a way through.*
- *Life is here to be enjoyed.*
- *I'm the sort of person who has great luck and a 'charmed life'.*
- *There is enough for everyone.*
- *Good people can get rich.*

Use any of these that apply to you and add your own. Now underline the three most powerful beliefs on each list. Notice how much effect they have in your life and how the negative or disempowering ones have held you back or made you unhappy. These are the beliefs that I am going to help you to eliminate, while strengthening and reinforcing the empowering beliefs and adding fresh ones that will support you in your goals.

HOW TO CHANGE YOUR BELIEFS

Changing your beliefs, or adding new ones, is absolutely possible and can happen in a remarkably short space of time. Beliefs that have governed your actions and thoughts for many years can be thrown out and new ones adopted in just a couple of weeks. The growth of hundreds of cults around the world is a clear, if alarming, example of how effectively people can be persuaded to adopt new beliefs. Some of the more damaging cults brainwash young people into rejecting their entire lives and families.

Be clear about what you want to believe and take responsibility for choosing your beliefs yourself. All it takes to confirm these new beliefs in your thinking is an understanding of the process involved and willpower. Here is my four step guide to changing your beliefs:

STEP ONE – WANT TO CHANGE

The essential first step in changing your beliefs is wanting to change. Beliefs are deeply personal and they shape the way you view your life. So they can be very hard to let go. Sometimes I find that a client is so attached to a belief that I have to prise it methodically from them before they can see that it's personal and not necessarily an absolute truth. If they're not willing to let go of the belief then it becomes almost impossible for me to help them achieve different and greater results.

DIRK'S STORY

DIRK WAS A YOUNG MAN WHO HAD SUPREME DIFFICULTY WITH EVERYTHING HE DID. WHEN HE LEFT SOUTH AFRICA TO COME TO LONDON FOR TWO YEARS TO WORK AS A RUGBY COACH HE ENCOUNTERED ENORMOUS SETBACKS AND PROBLEMS IN OBTAINING A VISA. YET HIS FRIENDS WHO'D DONE THE SAME THING HAD HAD NO PROBLEMS AT ALL. DIRK'S MOVE FROM LONDON TO NEW YORK HAD BEEN SIMILARLY FRAUGHT.

WHEN I QUESTIONED DIRK ABOUT HIS UNDERLYING ATTITUDES I FOUND HIS CHIEF BELIEFS ABOUT LIFE WERE: 1) NOTHING IS EVER

EASY; 2) WHATEVER YOU WANT IS WORTH FIGHTING FOR; 3) THE HARDER THE INPUT THE SWEETER THE RESULT; AND, 4) IT'S OUT THERE, GO GET IT, BUT IT'S HARD WORK.

DIRK DID BELIEVE HE WOULD SUCCEED, BUT HE ALSO BELIEVED THAT SUCCESS WOULD ONLY COME AT A HIGH PRICE AND THAT HE WOULD ENCOUNTER DIFFICULTY AND CONFLICT AND DO BATTLE EVERY STEP OF THE WAY. OF COURSE, BY THE AGE OF TWENTY-NINE DIRK HAD AMPLE EXPERIENCE AND EVIDENCE TO SUPPORT HIS BELIEFS. I WAS CURIOUS ABOUT THE ROOTS OF SUCH BELIEFS, BUT WHEN DIRK TOLD ME HIS STORY IT ALL BECAME CRYSTAL CLEAR. DIRK WAS BORN FIGHTING, HIS BIRTH WAS EXTREMELY DIFFICULT AND HE SURVIVED, BUT NOT WITHOUT A MAJOR STRUGGLE. LATER, FROM THE AGE OF FOUR, HE WAS BULLIED MERCILESSLY AT SCHOOL BECAUSE OF HIS 'BAT' EARS. HE SURVIVED BY FIGHTING BACK AND BEATING THE BULLIES. BY THIS YOUNG AGE DIRK ALREADY BELIEVED THAT HE WAS A FIGHTER AND A SURVIVOR, AND THIS BELIEF WAS TO SHAPE HIS LIFE. HIS DEMEANOUR FROM THEN ON WAS DEFENSIVE AND BELLIGERENT. SUCCEEDING THROUGH CHARM, HUMOUR OR DIPLOMACY WAS NEVER AN OPTION.

DIRK'S LIFE WAS ONE LONG SELF-FULFILLING PROPHECY. HE GOT EXACTLY WHAT HE EXPECTED AND HE KNEW EXACTLY HOW TO RESPOND. SHIFTING DIRK FROM HIS POSITION WAS IMPOSSIBLE, BECAUSE HE WAS HAPPY WITH HIS PERSPECTIVE; HE HAD SURVIVED SO FAR AND WOULD CONTINUE TO DO SO. HE COULD SEE THAT OTHERS AROUND HIM HAD A MUCH EASIER LIFE THAN HE DID, BUT HE ENJOYED DOING BATTLE TOO MUCH TO WANT TO GIVE IT UP.

What Dirk's story illustrates is that to want to change a belief you've got to see the advantages of changing it. You've got to be able to recognise that it isn't helping you. In fact, it may even be causing you enormous problems and you've got to be able to see that there's an alternative that could work for you in a far happier and more effective way.

STEP TWO – BELIEVE IT'S POSSIBLE

The next step in changing a belief is to open yourself to the possibility that it can be changed. In order for you to bring something new into your life or to move forward with any goal you have to allow that it is possible. I've often heard people say that they'd love to believe something different, but they just don't think it can be done. They see their current beliefs as facts – simply the way things are and unchangeable.

If this is you then you will now have to take the decision to suspend your disbelief. This is something I've talked about before, so you're already familiar with the idea. It doesn't mean you have actually to believe that changing your beliefs is possible. All you have to do is be willing to put your disbelief to one side and allow for the possibility that I am right about this. This will give you the space in which to be flexible and allow change.

Let me give you an example. I once coached a woman named Joan for a magazine article. I asked her to write a description of her ideal life, in one paragraph. What she wrote was so far removed from the sort of person she was that it was meaningless and simply told me that she did not believe in the possibility of living an ideal life. When we talked she confirmed this. She felt that one had to accept the hand of fate and that most things in life were out of her control. It took real effort on her part to begin to believe that she could actually make choices about the way she was living her life and begin to create the life she wanted.

Take a look at the guiding belief Oprah Winfrey has in her life: 'I don't think of myself as a poor deprived ghetto girl who made good. I think of myself as somebody who, from an early age, knew

I was responsible for myself and I had to make good.' These are the words of someone who is willing to take total responsibility for creating the life she wants with no excuses. It's all down to her – and no one and nothing else.

EXERCISE

Stop and ask yourself what your ideal life would look like. This need take no longer than about three minutes. If you don't do it right now then you have a lurking belief that your ideal life is not possible. If you take longer than three minutes you probably have a belief that says you can't come up with bright ideas easily and quickly!

Don't worry at this stage about the details. Just outline your ideal life, so that you can begin to acquire the habit of believing that what you truly want is possible.

Practise writing down your version of an ideal life every day for the next seven days – then keep these descriptions because we'll come back to them in a later chapter.

Here's a marvellous example of what belief can do. In May 1954 Roger Bannister ran a mile in 3 minutes 59.4 seconds. Reports of his astonishing achievement immediately flashed around the world. For the previous 100 years runners had tried unsuccessfully to run a mile in under four minutes. Anthony Robbins, in his book *Awaken the Giant Within*, and other scientists and doctors said that it couldn't be done. They claimed that the human heart would burst and that muscles and bones would tear and break under the stress of such an effort.

So what made it possible for Bannister to do the impossible? Why did he succeed where others had failed. The answer is quite simple. He chose to set aside the global belief that it wasn't possible and to believe in his goal.

It's even more interesting to look at what happened after Bannister set his record. Within seven months thirty-seven other runners had done it, too. In the next three years 300 more did it. How can this be explained? Had human physiology suddenly taken a quantum leap forward? Of course not. Any of the thirty-seven runners was as capable as Bannister of earning a place in the record books, but they were constrained by beliefs in a way that he was not. In his diary Bannister wrote:

> I prepared myself mentally in a very careful and concentrated fashion. I tried to establish this now or never attitude because I knew that unless I was successful in attaining this attitude I would perhaps lose my chance by letting myself fall prey to the mental reaction so common to athletes – that is, thinking that there would always be a next time of deciding, perhaps, that this is not the day.

How many of those thirty-seven runners had come close to succeeding before Bannister, but had passed up their chance by yielding to a limiting belief that 'this is not the day' or perhaps that it was too dangerous or not possible?

In every area of life the difference between being a record-breaker and one of the thirty-seven other runners who 'almost' did it can rarely be explained by a difference in skill or ability. In fact, the accolades often go to people with less ability. You may even know people who consistently get results, because what they lack in talent they make up for in desire and belief.

MARK AND JOHN'S STORY

I RECENTLY COACHED A SALES TEAM FOR AN IT COMPANY. MARK, ONE OF THE MOST SUCCESSFUL YOUNG MEN, WAS DETERMINED TO IMPROVE HIS PERFORMANCE EVEN FURTHER. HIS SELLING TECHNIQUES WERE FAULTLESS, SO I DECIDED TO TAKE A LOOK AT HIS BELIEFS

AROUND HIS JOB. *EUREKA!* WHEN I ASKED HIM TO TELL ME EVERYTHING HE KNEW AND BELIEVED ABOUT SELLING, ONE OF HIS COMMENTS WAS: 'FRIDAY IS A BAD DAY TO CALL CUSTOMERS.'

NOW IT DOESN'T MATTER HOW MANY TECHNIQUES I GIVE TO SOMEONE WHO BELIEVES THIS. THEY WILL SIMPLY NEVER BE AS SUCCESSFUL ON A FRIDAY BECAUSE THIS LIMITING BELIEF WILL OVERRIDE THEIR SKILLS. EVEN IF THEY HAD A GREAT DAY THEY WOULD DIMINISH THE RESULT BY SAYING SOMETHING ALONG THE LINES OF: 'WELL, I WAS LUCKY TODAY, BUT I BET I CAN'T DO THAT AGAIN NEXT WEEK.' WHEN MARK REALISED THE IMPACT OF HIS BELIEF, AND DECIDED TO CHANGE IT TO 'FRIDAY IS A GREAT DAY TO CALL CUSTOMERS,' HE GOT THE IMPROVED PERFORMANCE HE WAS AFTER.

ANOTHER YOUNG MEMBER OF THE SALES TEAM, JOHN, TOLD ME HE WANTED TO BE THE TOP SALESPERSON IN THE COMPANY. 'SO WHAT STOPS YOU?' I ASKED. 'I HAVEN'T BEEN WITH THE COMPANY LONG ENOUGH,' HE REPLIED. 'I NEED MORE EXPERIENCE.' ONCE THIS BELIEF HAD BEEN IDENTIFIED HE WAS ABLE TO CHALLENGE IT AND TO SEE THAT HIS LACK OF EXPERIENCE COULD EVEN BE AN ADVANTAGE, RATHER THAN A LIMITATION. AND, OF COURSE, IN THE LIGHT OF HIS NEW BELIEF HIS INEXPERIENCE — AND THE FRESH APPROACH HE BROUGHT WITH HIM — WERE AN ADVANTAGE TO HIM.

If you are willing to recognise those beliefs that limit you and to believe that it's possible to change them then you will open up a world of new and exciting possibilities for yourself. Give yourself the gift of identifying the chief limiting beliefs that lurk beneath the surface and hold you back.

STEP THREE – TAKE RESPONSIBILITY
If you want to make real changes you must begin by taking responsibility for the life that you have now and the beliefs that

have shaped it. There's absolutely no point in blaming circumstances or other people for your life now. Blame will simply keep you stuck and feeling like a victim.

Taking responsibility is liberating. It doesn't mean blaming yourself for whatever isn't working right now. It means recognising that you can choose to change it and to create the life you really *do* want. You don't need anyone or anything else to change; you don't have to depend on others or to wait for a lucky break. You can go out and make your own lucky break right now and go for what you want without holding back or feeling held back.

Taking responsibility means no more excuses. There's a great saying that I like to use: 'You can have what you want, or your reasons for not having it.' It really is that simple. Excuses are easy to make, but they're not a lot of fun when they're a substitute for action and success. So ditch the excuses and feel the buzz of knowing that the next step really is up to you.

To support yourself with this step look at the empowering beliefs that I asked you to write down earlier. Take the three strongest ones and recognise how they have helped you to achieve and succeed in your life so far. Decide to make them even stronger and more effective from this point on. See these beliefs as natural assets that will help you with whatever you have to face.

STEP FOUR – DISARM YOUR DISEMPOWERING BELIEFS
Look at the three most disempowering beliefs on the list I asked you to make earlier. Are you ready to confront and take issue with these beliefs? To stop them from limiting and controlling you? To refuse to pay the price they demand of you? Great!

It's time to question the validity of these beliefs – to pick them up, give them a good shake and begin to undermine the hold they have over you.

EXERCISE

Ask yourself the following questions about each of these negative beliefs:

1) *How is this belief ridiculous?*
2) *Who did I pick it up from? Do I still revere this person as I once did?*
3) *What does this belief cost me on a daily basis?*
4) *What will the long-term cost be if I don't let go of this belief?*

Asking these questions will begin to weaken these beliefs. I want you to feel the impact these beliefs have and to weaken them even further. Then decide to rid yourself of them forever.

Now take each belief and replace it with the opposite belief. For instance, if your disempowering belief was: 'At thirty-five I'm too old to change careers', replace it with: 'This is an ideal age to change careers; I will bring a wealth of talent and experience to a new job.'

I'm sure you get the idea. And coming up with your new beliefs is fun, especially if you make them as strong and empowering as possible. To weaken your disempowering beliefs further look for evidence to disprove them. Then look for evidence to prove your new beliefs. For instance, look for stories and examples of people starting new careers over the age of thirty-five.

When I do this with clients I ask them to look intensively for two weeks and to send me the proof of their new beliefs. During this time I am deluged with newspaper clippings, articles, surveys and research. The evidence was there all along, but my clients simply weren't looking for it. They were looking for evidence to support their old beliefs instead.

Remember that your beliefs have the meaning you give them. Make sure that you choose beliefs that are in line with the life you've chosen for yourself. With any step you want to take in life ask yourself what you would have to believe in order to succeed with it. And make your new beliefs stand out so much that others notice and comment on them. I decided to experiment with this when I chose to adopt the belief that I lead a charmed life. I simply chose this because it sounded so wonderful! I really focused on believing that this was the sort of person I naturally was. It took two weeks for someone to feed this belief back to me. In a conversation they said: 'Ah well, it's OK for you, you have a charmed life.' Needless to say I was absolutely delighted.

VICTORIA'S STORY

VICTORIA CAME TO ME BECAUSE SHE WANTED A SUCCESSFUL, LASTING RELATIONSHIP. VICTORIA WAS BRIGHT, FUN, AND WARM AND HAD A SUCCESSFUL CAREER, BUT HER RELATIONSHIPS WITH MEN HAD BEEN A DISASTER ZONE. SHE WAS A SINGLE PARENT WITH A SEVEN-YEAR-OLD DAUGHTER AND SHE HAD ONLY EVER HAD BRIEF AND UNSATISFYING RELATIONSHIPS WITH MEN. IF THEY DIDN'T DUMP HER WITHIN A FEW WEEKS, SHE DUMPED THEM.

WHEN WE TALKED I SOON REALISED THAT VICTORIA HAD ALL KINDS OF DAMAGING BELIEFS ABOUT MEN. HER FATHER HAD WALKED OUT ON THE FAMILY WHEN SHE WAS FIVE AND SHE'D BEEN LEFT WITH THE BELIEF THAT ANY MAN SHE GOT CLOSE TO WOULD ABANDON HER.

SHE SAW MEN AS AN ALIEN SPECIES: TO BE APPROACHED WITH CAUTION, HARD TO UNDERSTAND; AND ALMOST CERTAIN TO LET YOU DOWN. I POINTED OUT THAT THESE BELIEFS WERE BEHIND VICTORIA'S BEHAVIOUR AROUND MEN, WHICH INVOLVED EITHER CHOOSING MEN WHO WEREN'T REALLY INTERESTED AND WOULD LET HER DOWN, OR RUNNING A MILE IF A MAN ACTUALLY WANTED TO GET CLOSE TO HER. WE CAME UP WITH SOME NEW, HEALTHY BELIEFS FOR VICTORIA TO ADOPT AND SHE REJECTED HER OLD ONES AS RIDICULOUS AND UNTRUE. FOR SEVERAL WEEKS VICTORIA WORKED

HARD TO PUT HER NEW BELIEFS IN PLACE. EVERY DAY SHE'D LOOK
AT HERSELF IN THE MIRROR AND SAY: 'I HAVE A GREAT RELATIONSHIP
WITH A WARM, LOVING, HONEST, OPEN, ROMANTIC, GORGEOUS,
RESPONSIBLE AND COMMITTED MAN WHO ADORES ME.'

AFTER A MONTH VICTORIA PLACED AN AD IN THE DATING
COLUMN OF A MAGAZINE AND BEGAN DATING. SHE INSTANTLY
PASSED ON THE FIRST TWO MEN SHE DATED, RECOGNISING THAT
THEY WERE ONLY INTERESTED IN CASUAL RELATIONSHIPS AND
WEREN'T WHAT SHE WAS LOOKING FOR. THE THIRD MAN SHE MET
WAS THE ONE WHO FITTED HER NEW BELIEFS PERFECTLY. VICTORIA
IS NOW VERY HAPPILY MARRIED TO HIM, WITH A BABY SON.

WHAT DO YOU EXPECT?

You have already decided to cultivate beliefs that are aligned to
what you want in life. Now, to complete the picture, I want to
look at the expectations you carry round with you – which are
based on your beliefs – and project out on to the world. Like our
beliefs, expectations have a way of turning out exactly as we want
them to.

Look at these examples and see if any of them sound familiar:

- *Porsche drivers are so arrogant.*
- *Parking will be a nightmare.*
- *Men want younger women.*
- *Women want rich men.*
- *Life's so good at the moment, something's bound to go wrong.*
- *Accidents happen in threes.*
- *It's too good to be true.*

Ask yourself which two of your own expectations have come
true on a regular basis. You'll have lots to choose from because

we're all overflowing with expectations, some of which are trivial, others of which will shape your destiny. Remember that your world is personal; it is coloured by your perception and by all that you are conditioned to see, to select and to rationalise, so that your expectations will be fulfilled. The world that you live in is determined largely by what goes on in your mind.

Marcus Aurelius, the great Roman philosopher and sage said: 'A man's life is what his thoughts make of it.' Ralph Waldo Emerson, America's foremost philosopher, said: 'A man is what he thinks all day long.' Both of these men realised that the beliefs, thoughts and expectations that we habitually entertain will actualise themselves in the physical conditions of our world.

I once shared a house in a run-down area of London with five other students. The area had a high burglary rate and my house-mates were paranoid about being burgled. Our house resembled a fortress, with bars on the windows and barbed wire on the garden wall. And whose house was the most burgled in the area? Yes, ours, of course. My housemates even worked out when we could expect the next burglary, and sure enough, they were right.

When I moved out of that house I trained myself to expect only peace and security. I lived in the same neighbourhood for five more years with no bars on the windows or security devices and was not burgled once.

I remember speaking to an American client of mine about her contempt for English service in hotels, restaurants and shops. And I could see why she felt this way every time I was with her. Sure enough staff were singularly unhelpful wherever she went. Of course her rather haughty, imperious and irritable tone of voice didn't help; she projected her own annoyance, frustration and turmoil on to those around her and that's what she got back!

I suggested that she begin to expect great service, care and genuine kindness from the people with whom she came into contact in hotels and restaurants, and that she extend patience and be pleasant to them. She agreed to give it a go and instead of reacting in an angry and resentful way she began sending out loving thoughts and messages to waiting staff and shop workers and expecting people to be helpful and kind. This change in her own behaviour and expectation transformed her life, as she received excellent service wherever she went. As the writer Anaïs Nin wrote: 'We don't see things as they are, we see them as we are.'

GREAT EXPECTATIONS

I recently read with fascination of an experiment that was carried out with a class of nine-year-olds. A new teacher was told that a small group of these children were particularly gifted. The children knew nothing of this. At the end of term the 'gifted' pupils were found to have performed significantly better than the rest of the class. The teacher commented on how responsive she had found this group and how rewarding it was to teach them. Needless to say she was flabbergasted when she was told that the 'gifted' group was no more gifted than the rest of the class and had been picked at random. The selected group had performed better because she expected them to; her manner with them was one of heightened expectations and they rose to meet these expectations.

Think of your own schooldays. Did you meet your parents' and teachers' expectations, whether they were high or low? Were you expected to perform well in certain subjects? Our expectations of people shape the way we treat them and the way they respond.

One of my clients was a young, fast-growing company that was the talk of the industry. The staff were continually headhunted by rival companies because they performed so brilliantly. But whenever a member of staff did move to a rival company their performance was found to be disappointing. I asked the managing director why he thought this was. He didn't hesitate in his reply. He held his staff in the highest regard, he explained. He had the highest expectations of them and demonstrated his respect for them often and they responded by fulfilling those expectations. It really was as simple as that.

One of the reasons that my coaching clients get great results is that I expect them to. I demand the best from them and so they begin to demand the best from themselves. What a dreary and disappointing life would await us if we expected anything less than great things for ourselves. Expect the best, from life and from yourself.

EXERCISE

What are the five driving expectations of your life? How are you shaping your destiny right now with your expectations? Complete the following sentence:

One of my expectations about my life is . . .

Do this four times and then complete this sentence:

The strongest expectation I have about my life is . . .

If they're all great then *congratulations*, you're propelling yourself towards an exciting future. But if your expectations are propelling you towards a less than exciting future then it's time to change them.

Make sure that you check your expectations regularly – those relating both to everyday matters and bigger issues. Whether it's a parking space you're expecting or a new career, remember that your expectations will fulfil themselves.

EXPECT MORE

I want you to make the decision, today, to live with 'positive expectancy' in your life. Commit to positively expecting what you want and not what you don't want. Harness your phenomenal mind power and attract into your life the people, the responses and the outcomes that you want. By doing so you will be removing a great deal of the struggle and difficulty that most people encounter in their daily lives. Life doesn't have to be 'the way it is'. It can be the way you want it to be, if you're willing to make an unequivocal commitment to taking the steps necessary to get the results you want. The buck always has to stop with you. That's the deal. Don't make the mistake of beating yourself up or blaming yourself as you take this on. I am simply suggesting that you commit to taking more responsibility so that you can powerfully influence every area of your life.

If you want to test the power of expectation, try it out with parking spaces. I took the decision years ago to expect the best about parking and anticipate finding a parking space easily and effortlessly. I never mention this to the people I'm with, as I believe that if they expect to have difficulty parking it will undermine my own positive expectations. Nevertheless my passengers often marvel at my astounding good luck in just seeming to happen on a space just where I need it to be. Try it yourself. The next time you need a parking space suspend your doubts and see it clearly in your mind and expect it to be there. The better you get at this the better your results will be.

YOUR POSITIVE EXPECTANCY PLAN

Here's my five-step fail-proof plan for living with positive expectancy. Apply it rigorously, with enthusiasm, energy and optimism and then watch the results!

STEP ONE – BE VIGILANT

I want you to watch your every waking expectation, word and thought as closely as you can. Think through the consequences of each one. Weed out the feeble and lacklustre ones that lead you to disappointing results.

Remember that knowledge is power. If you go through your day and your life oblivious to the part you play in it you are severely handicapping your chances of creating the outcome you want. So be aware of what you say and do and create positive expectations for every situation.

For instance, if you go to a party, expect that people there will be delighted to see you. Expect them to want to talk to you and to like you. If you do, you will seem open, relaxed and inviting.

Carole Stone, once painfully shy and now Britain's best-connected networker and media queen, explains the queues of stars who attend her monthly parties and her success at bringing people together by saying: 'I always assume people are going to like me, not because I am wonderful but because I like them. I'm always slightly astonished if they say no, but I just wipe my nose and go off again.'

STEP TWO – GUARD YOUR CONCLUSIONS

We all form new expectations in response to events in our lives. It's important to be aware of these and to guard against taking on expectations that will create results you don't want. For example, if you have a bad experience with a builder working on your home, don't decide, as many people do, that all builders are cheats and can't be trusted. Don't generalise from one, or even two examples. Remember that there are many good and honest builders who do a great job and if you want to attract one of them next time, keep your expectations positive.

STEP THREE – STAY CHEERFUL

Staying cheerful and feeling happy, confident and optimistic about your future is a great goal. Yet, this approach is often dismissed as being unrealistic, as if it's a better option to expect problems and disappointment. But remember that what you expect creates your reality. So take the appropriate action to bring about the results you want and stay resolutely cheerful and focused on the positive outcome while you act.

Remember how much more you accomplish when you're feeling confident and energetic and firing on all cylinders? Training yourself to be the type of person who sees the glass as half full rather than half empty is actually the basis of cognitive therapy, the most popular and proven psychotherapeutic treatment for depression. Based on the common-sense view that depression is caused, in part, by mistaken thinking, the idea is to talk the patient out of the gloom using logic. If you believe yourself to be a total loser because you just failed your driving test the therapist will point out that this makes no sense because you have succeeded in other things. A patient will be encouraged to combat recurring despondent thoughts by systematically replacing them with optimistic ones. At least twenty authoritative studies have demonstrated the effectiveness of cognitive therapy, particularly in comparison to other forms of analysis and psychotherapy.

STEP FOUR – BE GRATEFUL

Cultivate an attitude of gratitude. Right now you have so many reasons to be cheerful. Think of ten of them right now. Appreciate your surroundings, your friends, the details of your life. It's so easy to concentrate on what's missing and what we don't have. But this attitude cultivates anxiety, which eats away at your health and your mental and emotional wellbeing. Gratitude does the opposite. It cultivates good health and a serene disposition, as well as being a lot pleasanter to experience.

We all know people who appear to be oblivious to the many riches in their lives – they see only what they haven't got and they don't appreciate it even when they get more. Choose not to be one of them. Get into the habit of being grateful for what you have right now.

This is a state of mind, an attitude that has nothing to do with how much or how little you have or what you have achieved. Every night before you go to sleep list at least twenty things for which you are grateful. It's a skill and practice perfects it. Soon you will think in this way all the time.

STEP FIVE – CHOOSE OPTIMISTIC FRIENDS

It is extremely difficult to maintain an upbeat, positive attitude towards life if you are constantly around people who do not have the same view. In fact, it's impossible. You don't have to abandon friends who are pessimistic and habitually expect the worst, but you do have to limit your time with them and increase your time with life's optimists. People rub off on you. Their attitudes affect you. As you become increasingly optimistic and enthusiastic you may well end up irritating those around you who don't share your approach. On the other hand, some may well decide they like your approach and decide to join in.

When I decided to change my way of thinking and way of life from a depressing no-hope perspective I moved away from everyone I knew. I was able to maintain a friendship with only one person and for some months I spent a great deal of time on my own. There was absolutely no other way in which I could break free of my old outlook while maintaining contact with people who held it.

Your situation is probably not as stark as this. Most people have a mixture of types among their friends. The point is that choosing the people you spend time with is important.

We all have a personal vibration, largely determined by the nature of our thoughts. As you work on yourself and consciously change your approach to life, your personal vibration will change. This is also known as your aura, an energy field surrounds the body. Sound cranky? It's not. A huge number of therapies have proved that it exists and it can even be photographed. Auras fluctuate and change, according to the nature of our thoughts and the state of our emotions and health at any given time. As you alter your outlook, your aura will change to reflect this. And as you retune your frequency you may find you are no longer on the same wavelength as someone else. This is why we grow apart from people and it also explains the strong pull we sometimes feel toward someone we have just met. We can tune in to them effortlessly; we gel.

Pessimistic people are always very draining. You are likely to feel inexplicably tired or down after spending time with them. Take a look around you and spot the people who are effective in life, who don't make hard work out of it and who are upbeat and resolutely cheerful. Bring more of this influence into your life.

YOUR ASSIGNMENT

Be your own soothsayer; foresee your own future. You have the power to divine results, far more than you had previously believed. See the connection between what you do now and what will happen in the future. Decide on some great expectations for yourself. Have faith in yourself and draw up a list of empowering beliefs and brilliant expectations for your life, both now and in the future.

Energise, validate and bring to life five of these beliefs and five of these expectations and, over the next month, make these part of your world. Predict and plan for your perfect destiny.

AND REMEMBER . . .

Beliefs have the potential to create or destroy.
Stop making excuses and take responsibility for your life.
If you want to live longer, be an optimist.
Choose beliefs that work and find evidence to prove them.
Believe you can do anything you want and you will.

CHAPTER SIX

WHAT DO YOU WANT AND WHAT ARE YOU GOING TO DO ABOUT IT?

LET'S REVIEW what we've been doing so far. We've already looked at your self-image, your self-esteem, your self-reliance and your beliefs and expectations about your life. We've looked at strengthening your internal resources and enhancing your psychological fitness.

I've spent some time laying this groundwork because self-belief, which encompasses all the aspects we've dealt with so far, is the master key to making real, profound and permanent changes in your life. To move through life without excessive struggle and turmoil you have to believe in yourself unequivocally. To take a giant leap forward – as you are about to do – you have to have generous stores of self-confidence and inner resources. Taking the necessary steps to create your ideal life requires a leap of faith, and a leap of faith requires confidence and courage.

Your destiny is shaped by your self-image because the way you see yourself determines your expectations. In turn your expectations determine your behaviour, which will create a particular outcome. In other words, the outcome you get will be the one you believe you deserve, and it will be in line with your self-image.

For example, if you see yourself as a winner you will expect great things for yourself and you will then persevere towards your goals, even when things get tough or challenging. Because of this you will succeed more often than you fail. Your successes confirm to yourself and everyone else that you are indeed a winner.

In contrast, if you see yourself as a loser you will expect little for yourself and give up easily when challenges come along. Because of this you will fail more often than you succeed and this will confirm the way you saw yourself all along – as a failure.

So, now that you've chosen to see yourself as a winner and created a gloriously confident self-image for yourself, it's time for the next stage: the challenge of defining your ideal life and then taking action to begin to live it.

As Thomas Jefferson, third President of the USA, once said: 'Nothing can stop a man with the right mental attitude from achieving his goal; nothing on earth can help a man with the wrong mental attitude.'

The better you feel about yourself the more adventurous your vision will be. A Big Plan requires you to be a Big Person with unlimited internal resources, loads of confidence and self-belief and the willingness to pick yourself up as many times as it takes to accomplish what you want. Life is so much more fun when we know that the only limitations are those of our own making. In that case, if you choose to set aside those limitations you can achieve absolutely anything you want to. In this chapter I am going to help make it clear what your ideal life looks like and then I am going to encourage you to take action to create it for yourself – right here, right now.

YOUR IDEAL LIFE

I want you to create a vision of your ideal life – a precise picture of the way you want to live, the people you want around you, the work you do, and the lifestyle you enjoy. Life is too short and too precious for you to waste it living a life that you don't enjoy, or that you see as a compromise. If it isn't fun and challenging then it isn't good enough for you. It's time to work out exactly what you need to change, to put in place or to create.

When you are living your ideal life, or taking the steps towards it, you will be making your own personal contribution to world peace and happiness. You will be adding your own contribution to the global pot. We talk about peace as though it's something outside our lives, out there in the world, something for politicians to create. But a state of peace and happiness begins inside each and every one of us. If you want to change the world, begin with yourself. Start with your own life. Make it what you want to see around you, both directly and globally. When you are living your ideal life you will be happier, healthier, more serene, have more energy, be more cheerful and look and feel years younger. You'll live longer because you'll love the way you live. I want you to map out a clear vision of every area of your life and clear goals for achieving your vision. It is nothing less than you deserve.

KNOW YOURSELF

To create a vision of what will genuinely make you happy you must be utterly honest and truthful with yourself. You need to know and to understand yourself well.

Don't fall into the trap of thinking that an ideal life is simply one in which you are fabulously wealthy, live in a huge house and drive a smarter car than anyone else. Plenty of people have all this and are still unhappy and unfulfilled.

The picture I want you to create is one in which life really works for you. Of course you may well include financial security, but this is just one factor. How do you want to spend your time? What drives you? What challenges excite you? I want you to think about a life in which you enjoy what you are doing and express your unique individuality. A balanced life, in which you have time for friends and family, relaxation, fitness and fun. A life free from the pressures that can lead to burn-out, exhaustion and illness. The time has passed when an ideal life simply meant more money. Many people are now choosing to turn their backs on high salaries when they are expected to work long hours under enormous pressure. They are realising that what matters far more is to enjoy life, to have good relationships and to be doing what you really want to do, rather than what you feel you ought to do.

As a wise man once said: 'Never get so busy making a living that you forget to make a life.' And making a life, it seems, is becoming increasingly important to more and more of us.

A recent report commissioned by Lloyds TSB, a UK bank, found that two-thirds of Britons would happily turn down extra salary gained from promotion if they could enrich their personal lives. The report said: 'It appears people would rather concentrate on building solid relationships and doing fun things than spending time in the office.'

The pursuit of material success is only one option. I want you to appreciate the many other options you have as well. So forget about your standing in the world and concentrate on your inner world. It will pay golden dividends.

A former dealer in the City (the centre of London's financial district), called Nick Probert, is a great example of someone who followed his heart and created his ideal life. As a foreign exchange dealer Nick was earning £250,000 a year. He had a big house, a

Ferrari and his two children went to private schools. But three years ago Nick, exhausted and burned out by the stress of his job and working extremely long hours, decided to quit his high-flying job.

Instead he became a painter and decorator, swapping his Ferrari for a small van and his huge salary for a modest £10,000 a year. He and his wife had to sell their home and take their children out of private school, but they have no regrets.

Nick says: 'I was a success, but I was a stranger in my own home. Giving up my job was the best move I ever made. Crazy as it sounds I think I'm more of a success than I ever was before. My perception of success, my career, wasn't bringing happiness to me or to my family. Now I see how little it meant to my children having a father who had an important job if he was never at home.'

Nick reorganised his priorities and found the courage to live his ideal life. We are living in exciting times of change when more and more of us are questioning our priorities and realising that we have so much choice about the way we live. Many people are redefining their ideas about life and what really is ideal.

I have had a number of clients who have feared the loss of prestige that giving up a high-flying job would involve. The only answer is to look beyond what others think and make your opinion of yourself the one that counts.

As Martin Luther King Junior said: 'If a man is to be called a street sweeper he should sweep streets even as Michaelangelo painted or Beethoven composed music. He should sweep streets so well that all the hosts of heaven and earth will pause to say, here lived a great street sweeper who did his job well.'

Stop, right now, and give yourself the gift of imagining your ideal life. Put aside your judgements and questions and write it down, in no more than ten lines. Don't worry about the details at this stage, because this is just the first draft.

TIME TO GROW UP

Throughout this book I have emphasised the importance of consciously taking more responsibility for your results in life, and of choosing the type of person you want to be and your attitude to life. Now I want you to take this a stage further, by taking total responsibility for actively creating the specific results you want. To do this is a huge challenge because it involves being truly grown-up. When you grow up, in the fullest sense, you give up all blame towards anyone else for any dissatisfaction you may feel about your life. You become your own person and don't need the approval of your parents, or anyone else, for the way you choose to live.

I have coached successful people in their thirties and forties who have yet to grow up in this full sense. Some of them are adult men and women who resist the challenge of living their own lives, choosing rather to live in the shadow of their parents or family and to live a life that is ideal in someone else's eyes, but not necessarily their own.

I have known grown men and women who still harbour grudges against their parents or teachers for not giving them the right encouragement or the right start in life. I point out to them that they were with their parents for only the first eighteen or so years of their lives and that they've had at least twenty years of being in charge of their own lives.

As an adult you can give yourself whatever you missed out on as a child. You can become your own parent and your own champion, defining your own meaningful life. To make the decision to stand on your own two feet, blaming no one; to make your own decisions and live with the consequences; and, to take total responsibility for your life, is a fantastic and truly grown-up step to take.

Myths often reflect profound truths about human nature and psychology and the myths of different cultures often have great similarities. One of the most common, found in almost every culture, is the myth of the hero's journey, in which the hero sets out in pursuit of his destiny. There are always terrifying obstacles to be overcome on his path, symbols of the rites of passage and challenges that every human being faces on the way to self-realisation.

The hero always has to leave his family, often sadly and with a painful parting. This is a reflection of a universal truth: in order to become who you are going to be, you must leave behind your beginnings.

Sometimes the hero returns to his family, changed and enriched, and when this happens in real life, as it often does, the relationship is subtly altered so that the former child returns as an equal to his parents. All growth involves saying goodbye, in order to say hello. Leaving, whether it is the womb of family, an unhappy but familiar relationship, or a secure but dull job may seem difficult, but very often one part of life has to be released before a fresh one can take its place.

Remember that in growing up and choosing your own life path you are setting out on your own hero's journey, with all the challenges, discoveries, partings and triumphs that it will bring. By growing up you will set yourself free.

EXERCISE

How grown-up are you? How free are you to make decisions that reflect what you really want out of life and demonstrate who you really are? Do you still blame or resent your parents or other influential figures from your childhood?

Complete the following statements. If it feels appropriate then do the exercise twice, once for each parent. You can also do it for other significant figures in your life or for your school.

1) *I blame my parents for . . .*
2) *I resent my parents for . . .*
3) *I can't forgive my parents for . . .*
4) *What I wish they'd done is . . .*
5) *The effect on my life has been . . .*

This exercise will be illuminating because most of us still harbour childhood resentments and grudges. Make a decision, right now, to let them go, because all they do is hold you back and prevent you from taking responsibility for your life, and making it the life you want. For each blame, resentment or grudge complete this statement:

I now choose to forgive my parents for . . .

However bad your start in life, it is now time to move beyond it and to cut any remaining umbilical ties that connect you to it. When you consciously break these ties by forgiving and letting go then you are free to move on. Remember that your parents were doing the best they could with the resources they had. Blaming them now is pointless.

Ask yourself this: *If I took total responsibility for creating my own happiness and the life I want then what changes would I make?*

List five changes you would make.

Now decide to activate one of these changes, right now. Do something about it today and make it a priority to begin making this change over the next seven days.

NO MORE EXCUSES

No matter what hand you've been dealt in life, it's up to you to make the best of it and to begin making your life the best it can be. I came across two people recently who very clearly demonstrated the difference in attitude between blaming others for disadvantages and taking full responsibility for creating an ideal life.

Justine worked for me a few years ago and was responsible for the smooth running of a very busy operation. She was a delightful person, but prone to being scatterbrained. When I asked her about this she laid the blame entirely on her parents! No kidding. She explained that her life was blighted by the fact that her parents had sent her to a 'progressive' Rudolph Steiner school, where she believed there wasn't enough discipline and order. This was combined with a relaxed, Bohemian home life and Justine felt that her disorganised style was the result. She was stuck with it for life! Or so she felt. Yet Justine was twenty-six and had absolute choice, at this stage, about whether to stay disorganised or learn to organise herself better.

Shehwar Shah, on the other hand, was a young man who had grown up with a truly disadvantaged childhood. He and his brothers and sisters were terrified of his father, who walked out and left his mother with heavy debts and four children to raise. She worked as a seamstress and there was very little money. Shehwar was twelve when he began stealing and at the age of seventeen he was convicted of robbery and sentenced to three and a half years in a young offenders' institution.

For the first few months Shehwar lay on his bunk, miserable and alone, listening to a torrent of racist abuse from the other prisoners. But a year into his sentence Shehwar decided to do something with his life. He began studying and within eighteen months he had six GCSEs and two A levels. After that he got a place at university to study psychology and criminology, which he took up as soon as he left prison.

'I never want to go back to prison,' he says, 'but being sent there was the best thing that could have happened because it was there that I learned what I was capable of doing.'

Now Shehwar, at twenty-two, is studying and dreaming of marriage and a family. And his mother, having brought up all her children, is now studying law. Shehwar, arguably, had all the cards stacked against him. He could have chosen the route of self-pity, of one crime after another or of blaming everyone around him. Instead he chose to take responsibility, to grow up and to make a great life for himself.

Like Justine and Shehwar you have choices and you can either make excuses or get on with having a good life.

BELIEVE IT'S POSSIBLE

If someone like Shehwar can turn his life around, without bitterness or self-pity, then anyone can. Shehwar is on his path, living his ideal life. Are you? And if not, why not? Clients are often bewildered when I ask them this question. They think I'm either joking or being a fantasist and they're stunned when they realise that I'm absolutely serious. So many of us have such limited horizons. We have been conditioned to think in such rigid ways that to contemplate an ideal life is dismissed as 'building castles in the sky' or having a 'Pollyanna' attitude.

What have you decided is impossible in your life? What have you told yourself is beyond your reach? Where have you drawn the line between what's possible and what isn't? How resigned are you to putting up with certain aspects of your life? Which aspects are they?

In order to make changes you must begin to believe that anything is possible and to re-draw that line between the possible and the impossible. You can change your job, your home, your relationship, your stress levels, your way of approaching life or your health. Begin by allowing yourself to believe, today, that what you want is possible, reachable and that you deserve it.

RICHARD'S STORY

RICHARD CAME TO ME WHEN HE WAS MADE REDUNDANT BY THE PROPERTY INVESTMENT COMPANY FOR WHICH HE WORKED. FOR YEARS HE HAD YEARNED TO WORK FOR HIMSELF AND HAD FELT DEEPLY UNFULFILLED IN THE WORK HE WAS DOING. HIS REAL DREAM WAS TO TURN DERELICT BUILDINGS IN UP-AND-COMING AREAS OF LONDON INTO STYLISH ART AND LEISURE CENTRES.

I COULD SEE INSTANTLY HIS GENIUS FOR SPOTTING THE PERFECT LOCATION, BUYING AT THE RIGHT TIME, BRINGING TOGETHER THE PERFECT MIX OF INVESTORS AND MANAGING THE ENTIRE PROJECT FROM START TO FINISH. HIS ENTHUSIASM WAS INFECTIOUS AND HIS FLAIR OBVIOUS. RICHARD WAS ABSOLUTELY CLEAR ABOUT WHAT HE WANTED, YET HE TOLD ME HE THOUGHT HE HAD AS MUCH CHANCE OF GETTING IT AS HE HAD OF WINNING THE LOTTERY.

RICHARD'S FANTASY WAS TO FIND A COMPANY OR INDIVIDUAL WHO SHARED HIS VISION AND WHO COULD AFFORD TO SET HIM UP IN A GOOD OFFICE IN CENTRAL LONDON, WITH FULL ADMIN SUPPORT, PAY HIM A GOOD SALARY, GIVE HIM A SHARE IN THE COMPANY AND COMMISSION ON DEALS AND THEN ALLOW HIM COMPLETE FREEDOM TO FIND THE SITES AND TRANSFORM THEM.

BUT HE DIDN'T SEE HOW THIS COULD HAPPEN IN THE 'REAL' WORLD. SO I ASKED HIM TO SUSPEND HIS DISBELIEF, TREAT HIS DREAM AS A REAL POSSIBILITY AND DO EVERYTHING HE COULD TO FIND THE COMPANY OR INDIVIDUAL HE WAS LOOKING FOR.

WITHIN A MONTH HE HAD SPOTTED AN ADVERTISEMENT IN A PROPERTY JOURNAL. A SMALL CONSORTIUM WAS LOOKING FOR SOMEONE WITH RICHARD'S EXPERIENCE AND QUALITIES. HE COULD HARDLY BELIEVE WHAT HE WAS READING. OVER LUNCH IN ONE OF LONDON'S EXCLUSIVE HOTELS RICHARD MET HIS NEW PARTNER, A MAN WHO HAD SOLD A SUCCESSFUL BUSINESS AND WHO NOW SPENT MOST OF HIS TIME IN SPAIN, BUT WHO WAS VERY INTERESTED IN

COMMERCIAL PROPERTY DEVELOPMENT IN LONDON.

THE DEAL WAS STRUCK AND RICHARD NOW OPERATES HIS BUSINESS FROM A SMART ADDRESS IN CENTRAL LONDON. HE RECEIVES A GENEROUS SALARY, HAS A 25 PERCENT STAKE IN THE COMPANY, MAKES COMMISSION ON DEALS AND HAS ALL THE CONTROL AND FREEDOM HE WANTED.

YET CHANCES ARE THAT RICHARD WOULD NEVER HAVE SEEN THAT AD IF HE HADN'T BEEN WILLING TO BELIEVE THAT HIS PERFECT OUTCOME WAS POSSIBLE.

CLEAR OUT THE OLD

Before you begin the business of ushering new ideas, things and people into your life it's essential to make some room for them. And that means getting rid of what you no longer use, need, like or have room for. If you were redesigning your home you'd remove all the old, outdated stuff before bringing in new furniture. It's the same with your life. Clutter, whether physical or emotional, takes up space and blocks the way for new things in your life. So be ruthless about letting go of what you no longer need.

Put your house in order. It's impossible to think clearly when you're surrounded by physical clutter. Look around you. Are there piles of books, videos, CDs, letters, papers, clothes you no longer wear and knick-knacks you've collected? All of these sap your energy. Put aside a day for clearing and go through every room, area and cupboard as well as your garage or shed. Sell, give away or throw away what you no longer need. We wear, on average, only 15 percent of the clothes in our wardrobes. If you haven't worn something for a year, get rid of it.

Doing this will leave you feeling energised and ready to move on. Revel in having less, don't just re-fill the space. Surround yourself only with the objects that delight you.

Now move on to your work environment and do the same, whether you work at home, have your own office or simply have a desk and a space in a larger office. Keep your working area clean and clear. Make sure you can instantly lay your hands on anything you need.

After you've finished with your home and your work, move on to your life. What or whom do you need to say no to? What or whom do you tolerate or put up with? Is it time to end a relationship with someone who drains and exhausts you? Or to leave a job? Or to refuse favours you've been feeling obliged to do? Sometimes the clutter in your life is harder to pinpoint than the physical clutter in your home. But it's just as important to clear it. You may feel fearful at the idea, but you'll also feel enormous relief.

EXERCISE

Complete the following statement:

Something I'm willing to say no to in my life right now is . . .

Repeat this five times, and more if you need to.

Now take the most straightforward item on your list and prioritise it. Begin clearing it from your life right now. Do whatever you need to do to say no to it and then remind yourself of this commitment every day. It may be something you need to say no to repeatedly, such as a habit. So back yourself up by writing every day:

I am no longer tolerating . . .

If it's a habit, it may take a few weeks to break, but persevere and you will break it. If it's a deeper issue, such as unhappiness at work or in a relationship, then you will need to plan a course of action for yourself. The very act of defining what isn't working and writing it down has already started you on the path to change. All you need to do is to follow it, one step at a time.

ANDREA'S STORY

ANDREA CAME TO ME COMPLAINING ABOUT HER ACTION-PACKED, CLUTTERED LIFE. SHE DIDN'T HAVE A MINUTE TO HERSELF AND SHE NEEDED TO EARN SOME EXTRA MONEY TO FIX THE ROOF ON HER HOME. ANDREA WAS HAPPILY MARRIED WITH A SON OF NINE. SHE DIDN'T HAVE A JOB, BUT SHE HAD CREATED A LIFE WHERE SHE WAS RUNNING ROUND IN CIRCLES TRYING TO KEEP UP WITH ALL HER COMMITMENTS. ANDREA COULDN'T SAY NO TO ANYONE OR ANYTHING; SHE WAS A COMPULSIVE DO-GOODER. SHE DID THE CHURCH ACCOUNTS, RAN THE SCHOOL PTA, HELPED OUT IN THE SCHOOL OFFICE AND DID THE SCHOOL RUN FOR SEVERAL OTHER PARENTS.

ANDREA CLEARLY HAD TO LEARN TO SAY NO, BUT THE IDEA FILLED HER WITH GREAT ANXIETY. IN FACT, SHE DIDN'T EVEN HAVE THE VOCABULARY TO SAY NO. SHE HAD NO IDEA HOW TO GO ABOUT IT. I HAD TO TEACH HER THE WORDS AND PHRASES SHE MIGHT USE.

GRADUALLY ANDREA BEGAN TO PUT THESE INTO USE AND TO CLEAR HER LIFE. SHE TOLD THE OTHER PARENTS SHE COULD NO LONGER MANAGE THE SCHOOL RUN EVERY DAY AND SUGGESTED A ROTA INSTEAD, WHICH FREED HER ON THREE MORNINGS A WEEK. SHE OFFLOADED SOME OF HER MANY RESPONSIBILITIES AND WAS DELIGHTED TO DISCOVER THAT OTHER PEOPLE WEREN'T ANGRY WHEN SHE DID SO. MOST OF THEM ACCEPTED IT QUITE HAPPILY.

THE RELIEF ANDREA FELT WAS VAST AND SHE WAS ABLE TO CLEAR HER LIFE ENOUGH TO FIND A PART-TIME JOB AND EARN THE MONEY FOR HER NEW ROOF, AS WELL AS PUTTING SOME TIME ASIDE, REGULARLY, FOR HERSELF.

WHY SET GOALS?

Why bother to set goals? Doesn't it take some of the fun out of life, the element of surprise, of waiting to see what's around the corner? Or of trusting in fate to bring you whatever you're meant to have in life? I am often asked these questions, so let's clear this one up right now. We all set goals, whether we do it consciously or not. You are living your goals right now. Whatever you're doing, whatever you are in life is the result of decisions you've made earlier and actions you've decided to take or not take.

What I want is for you to have clear, conscious, up-front choices in your life, rather than the backdoor type of choices by which so many people live. So many people say they don't know what they want out of life in a year or five years' time. They have only a vague notion of where they're going. And this becomes their decision about life, to drift through in a vague haze, blaming someone or something else if they don't like the way things turn out.

I want you to move into the driving seat and take yourself where you really want to go. I want you to enjoy the journey and to look forward to arriving at your various destinations.

Being a backseat passenger in your own life isn't good enough for you. Instead, decide to give your all to your life, to live it to the full and to appreciate how precious it is. If you need any more evidence to fuel your resolve then talk to elderly people who are nearing the end of their lives. What most of them will tell you is: 'Don't take life for granted, don't waste a minute; take chances and enjoy everything.' They'll tell you of the things they didn't get round to doing or seeing and all the things they'd do if they had their time over again. To look back and regret wasted chances and missed opportunities is heartbreaking, yet so many people do. Choose now not to be one of them.

My view of goal-setting is simply that it gives you an

131

opportunity to have clear vision in your life, to take yourself and your life seriously and to choose what you want in life. To leave your life and your future to fate is to avoid taking full responsibility for yourself and for life's challenges.

Religion is often used to justify inaction and divine intervention is used as an excuse for avoiding change. Yet the idea that God will rush in when the time is right is selfish and absurd. The *bible* says that God helps those who help themselves and it is full of stories of wise and exemplary people using the opportunities they've been given. Enlisting outside help, divine or otherwise, is invaluable in achieving goals. But that's very different to sitting back and waiting for God, Lady Luck or anyone else to come knocking at the door.

My experience is that when you get clear about your goals and begin taking action yourself, you attract support and assistance of all kinds along the way. Goëthe, the nineteenth-century philosopher, put this beautifully when he said:

> Until one is committed there is hesitancy, the chance to draw back, always ineffectiveness. Concerning all acts of initiative there is one elementary truth, the ignorance of which kills countless ideas and endless plans. That the moment one definitely commits oneself then providence moves too. All sorts of things occur to help one that would never otherwise have occurred. A whole stream of events issue from the decision, raising in one's favour all manner of unforeseen incidents and meetings and material assistance which no man could have dreamed would come his way. Whatever you can do, or dream you can, begin it. Boldness has genius, power and magic in it. Begin it now.

Throughout this book I have urged you to write out your goals and there's an important reason for this. It not only makes them clearer, but it makes them seem real and greatly increases your chances of achieving them. Here's a stunning illustration of why.

Back in 1979, Harvard University did a study. They asked their graduates at the Harvard Business School the following question: 'How many of you have clear, written goals and have made plans to accomplish them when you leave this school?'

Three percent had written goals, 13 percent had unwritten goals and 84 percent had no goals at all. Ten years later they went back to find out how they were doing. The three percent who'd written out their goals were earning, or were worth, ten times as much as the other 97 percent.

When you have clear goals you move towards them automatically. You become like a guided missile; you receive feedback and then stay on course or adjust as necessary, but you always have those goals within your vision.

Think of the carrier pigeon. You can take it a thousand miles from its home and it will still make its way, unerringly, back to where it came from. Think of yourself and your goals in the same way. You know what you have to do to get there and you are on your journey, flying clearly and swiftly to where you want to be.

THE GOOD GOAL-SETTING GUIDE
Here's my guide to setting your goals in a clear and effective way.

KEEP YOUR GOALS CONFIDENTIAL
It is crucial to keep your goals confidential. You dilute and weaken your drive and momentum when you talk about them too much. Your energy goes into talking about your goals rather than achieving them and you open yourself to discouraging reactions. Only share them with someone who is on the same path and who has goals of their own to pursue. Not everyone will share your

quest for success; in fact, some people may react against it as it alerts them to their own dissatisfaction and insecurity. Bette Midler once said: 'The only problem with success is finding people who are happy for you.' She was talking about mega-success Hollywood-style, and when you're successful on that level then you tend to have a very small circle of close friends – the ones who genuinely are happy for you.

BUILD A SUCCESS NETWORK

Search out and find the right people with whom to surround yourself. Dr David McClelland of Harvard University spent twenty-five years researching success and achievement and his conclusion was this: your reference group, the people with whom you associate on a regular basis, largely determines your success or failure in life. His conclusion was that 90 percent of everything that happens to you in life will be determined by the people you associate with on a daily basis. You begin to think, walk, act, dress and talk like them, and you share the opinions of people you are around most of the time. So associating with like-minded people is vital to making successful changes. Select your relationships with care. I recommend you seek out two or three people to form a small success group, with the intention of giving each other support and solidarity and of celebrating each other's successes. Call it whatever seems right, your goal group or momentum group, for instance. Then draw up some rules, keep it closed, confidential and consistent and make it fun by meeting in great places. It's a wonderful feeling to have others rooting for you.

MAKE YOUR GOALS SMART

Your goals need to be SMART – that is, Specific, Measurable, Ambitious, Realistic (watch this one!) and Timed. So, for example, it's no good having a goal to be 'happier'. You need to define what this would mean for you: maybe working fewer hours or having more time for yourself, etc. Then work out the detail of what this would involve – more time for yourself might mean half an hour a day, or an hour three times a week. With this kind of clarity you can begin to plan for what you want and to work out a time scale in which to achieve it.

Don't let realistic become an excuse for keeping your goals timid. Make them brave and ambitious. Make sure that whatever goal you aspire to is one that you truly believe you can attain, even though you know you'll have to stretch yourself to get there.

GET EXCITED

Your goals must get you excited, otherwise you won't have the drive and motivation to achieve them. You'll know they're exciting enough when you experience a surge of energy and a renewed optimism. Even if you wake up in the night brimming with ideas, you'll still have the energy to see you through the next day because the excitement carries you through.

I remember calling my brother Brian at 9.30 one evening to find him still at work. 'Aren't you tired?' I asked him. 'Why would I be tired?' he replied. 'If I was at a party now I wouldn't feel tired, I'd be having a great time, so why should I feel tired now?' Needless to say, Brian loves his work.

Exciting goals will fuel your imagination. You'll come up with ideas and options you would never have considered without them. I recall one new client complaining that he had great difficulty getting out of bed in the morning. He asked whether I could help. My answer was simple: we'd come up with good reasons for him to get out of bed. It was nothing to do with willpower, simply exciting reasons to get up. Marcus Aurelius, the Roman emperor and philosopher, wrote: 'It is not death that man should fear, but he should fear never beginning to live.'

EXERCISE

Ask yourself these questions:

1) *What would you do and how would you change your life if you won the lottery tomorrow. OK, what would you do after that long holiday?*
2) *What have you always wanted to do in life but been afraid to attempt?*
3) *What activities, throughout your life, have given you the greatest feeling of achievement?*
4) *What would you do if you knew you couldn't fail?*
5) *What are your three most important goals in life right now?*
6) *What would you do, how would you spend your time if you learned that you had only six months to live?*
7) *If your life was perfect in every respect and you were too, what would it look like?*

Great. Now you've got a clear idea of the life you would like to be living and the goals you want to work towards.

YOUR PERSONAL GOALS

Right, it's time to get some exciting goals down on paper. Let's go back to that ideal life scenario I asked you to sketch out earlier in this chapter. Read through it and then start again, using it as the basis of a longer, more thorough description. Remember that your goals have to be challenging but realistic and believable for you. You also need short-term goals and long-term goals.

First of all, spoil yourself by including what you'd really, really like in your life and call this list: 'My Five Dream Goals'. Think of these as total treats and put in a date or an age by which you'd like to have them.

Now take as long as you want to describe your ideal life. Brainstorm and put down everything that comes to mind, in no particular order. Resist being precious and too detailed at this stage. When you've finished, go back and see what categories you can identify. My suggestions are: health and fitness, career, finances, family, professional, social and community.

Put everything into these separate compartments. Now extend your list to ten goals for each area.

When you've done this, take out the five most exciting ones from each category and write them out again. Taking action on too many goals at once will overwhelm you and spread your energy too thinly. Now take each goal and decide where you'd like to be with it in three years' time, then one year's time, six months, three months, one month and one week's time.

If you could only achieve one goal from each category, which one would it be? Mark these out and give them preferential treatment and extra attention. These are your VIGs (very important goals). Then give all the others a rating – second, third and so on.

TAKE ACTION

Now is the time to take action – immediately and decisively. Then you'll be on your way. You're training yourself to be action-oriented and learning what it feels like to be truly alive and awake to your true potential. You're on track and in the driving seat.

Action is vital. It's easy to dream about goals while doing nothing and planning to so something tomorrow. Do something right now – today – and you're on the way to success.

Review your goals every night and read through them first thing in the morning. Once a week update your position so that you have a new week's action plan. Make sure you reach each week's goals and tick them off as you reach them.

Update your goals for each month, too, as well as every year. Don't be afraid to be flexible. You can change your mind, adapt and change direction as you see fit.

Remember that your ultimate goal is happiness. The process of goal-setting is not about putting off and planning happiness, but about achieving happiness right now, by knowing that you're on your way and by having a plan that is materialising day by day, and satisfying, fulfilling and exciting you. I want to increase your store of happiness, both now and in the future.

Finally, if you falter, consider this quote from American Indian Clearwater: 'Do not come to the end of your life only to find you have not lived. For many come to the point of leaving the earth and when they gaze back, they see the joy and the beauty that could not be theirs because of the fears they lived.'

Fortune smiles on the brave. When you step out as one of the elite, living in a fearless way, you can afford to feel that you are one of the few in this world who stand out a mile, who are totally awake and alert, who are really living.

YOUR ASSIGNMENT

Today I want you to do something to get started on every one of your primary goals. Make a call, join a gym, set up a meeting, start investigating possibilities, talk to the right person, whatever you need to do, but *take action* and make it happen.

After that I want you to take action every day towards your goals, refusing to falter, hesitate, doubt or give in. If you are willing to take immediate and continuous action then you can't fail.

Go do it!

AND REMEMBER . . .

You need to know what your ideal life is in order to live it.

Choose to see yourself as a winner who doesn't give up.

Give up blaming anyone or anything else for whatever goes wrong in your life.

Pick yourself up and carry on as many times as you need to.

Make clear, conscious choices about how you want your life to be.

Take action to make your goals real.

CHAPTER SEVEN

Do the Work You Love and Love the Work You Do

WHAT I want you to look at in this chapter is your working life. For many people work is a drudge, a part of the day to be endured and put up with. For others work is all right but nothing special. It passes the time, brings in the money and OK they don't love it, but they don't hate it either. Only a small and hugely fortunate percentage of people love what they do, waking up each day and looking forward to work and all the satisfaction and rewards it brings them. These people know what it's like to feel deeply fulfilled, to have a purpose, to make a difference and to live every part of their lives fully. This doesn't mean, of course, that they're workaholics or that work takes over their lives. Work should never be all of your life, or even the biggest part of it. But work should be valuable.

Working is not simply about earning a living, or even doing something useful. Valuable, satisfying, enriching work is vital to the wellbeing of the human soul. To work is natural and normal, not a burden imposed on us by society. To do satisfying work is to know your own value and to know that you are making a contribution to the lives of others as well as your own.

To avoid work when you are capable of it, or to do work that you simply endure, is to ignore your own ability and potential and to waste your talents and resources.

If you don't like the job you are doing then you are doing the wrong job. It's as simple as that. It's easy to justify staying in the wrong job with all sorts of reasons. Here are some of the most common ones people use: the money's good, it's convenient, it's a family business, I'll never get another job, I'm used to it.

There are many excuses you can use to stay where you are, but if your job doesn't thrill and excite you then these are just excuses for avoiding your true purpose and potential.

EXERCISE

Take pen and paper and write the answers to the following questions. Don't think about them, just put down whatever comes into your mind.

1) *The things I love about my job are* . . .
2) *The things I hate about my job are* . . .
3) *I'm in my job because* . . .
4) *The talents I use in my job are* . . .
5) *The talents I don't use in my job are* . . .

The results will give you a clear indication of whether you're in the right job or not. If the plusses don't outweigh the minuses by at least ten to one then your job is not ideal for you.

WHY YOU NEED TO WORK

However well intentioned, the modern welfare state, with it's vast array of social benefits, has spread the malaise of chronic dependency that has stunted the lives of vast numbers of able people. Too many people believe that it is acceptable and even their right to depend on the state to support them. And the disastrous consequence of this for each one of those people has been the weakening of self-reliance, the erosion of self-belief and self-worth and the growing belief that they're useless and unfit for anything.

When we begin to depend on institutions and outside help to support us then we destroy our potential for success and fulfilment. The Scottish writer Samuel Smiles, writing as long ago as 1866 in his best-seller *Self Help*, put it perfectly when he said: 'Help from without is often enfeebling in its effects, but help from within invariably invigorates. Whatever is done for men of classes, to a certain extent takes away the stimulus and necessity of doing for themselves; and where men are subjected to over-guidance and over-government the inevitable tendency is to render them comparatively helpless.'

Today things are changing, as successive governments in both Britain and the USA are recognising the massive deficiencies of the welfare state and are putting policies in place to force people back to relying on their own resources.

Several states in the USA have adopted a 'sink or swim' policy, by withdrawing welfare payments after two years. Critics predicted a social disaster, with hundreds of families ending up on the streets, but this hasn't happened. Families have rallied round, jobs have been found, people have fallen back on their own resources and found solutions.

I am not for one moment suggesting that we should abandon societal responsibility for those who are truly in need. The vulnerable, the sick, the elderly and the very young must be cared for. And we could be far more generous to these sections of the community by refusing to give income to able people who could be working. With their basic needs met by the state, without the real need to work and without the incentive to take action so many people are existing in a helpless and often hopeless condition.

British public opinion is increasingly intolerant of this dependency. The UK's most popular soap opera *Coronation Street* ran a storyline about a character, Les Battersby, who was claiming to be unemployed and drawing state benefits while doing part-time work on the side. Before the storyline ran, 2,000 people a week were reporting those they knew who were doing just this. After the story appeared the figure rose to 4,000, where it has remained.

Some cultures – including Jewish and Asian cultures – emphasise self-reliance and the capacity for hard work as vitally important characteristics. Both these groups are prepared to work long and hard to establish themselves and to provide for themselves and their families. Both consider it a duty for families to provide for each other. In these cultures children are surrounded by positive examples of self-reliance, enterprise and hard work.

The difference between these cultures, with their thriving and positive belief in work, and so many sectors of Western society – where work has become unknown and only lethargy and depression thrive – is obvious. Work matters, and not just because of the need to earn an income. As Body Shop founder Anita Roddick points out so clearly in her book *Trade not Aid*, what people need is the means to help and support themselves, not just hand-outs. To feel good about yourself, to feel worthwhile and a functioning member of society you need to work.

No excuses

Plenty of people are out of work because they have been made redundant or been sacked or they've been through some other circumstance of life. We live in a hugely ageist society where many companies consider employees past it once they turn forty. Many jobs are only open to those under thirty-five and large numbers of hugely talented and experienced people over forty can't find work. Don't join this mindset. Refuse to label yourself by age or to accept this kind of limited thinking.

Penny Smith, a GMTV presenter, once said: 'I think thirty-eight is the perfect television age. I have no intention of ever getting to forty-two. In ten years time I will still be thirty-eight.' And employed as a TV presenter, no doubt.

Refuse to see yourself as someone who is too old for a job. If you are rejected because of your age, or any other factor beyond your control, then set up in business for yourself. Even if you haven't worked for years you can go out and get a job tomorrow. Look the part, smile, be the age you feel you are, forget about your birth certificate and expect to be given the job. If you're still working towards your ideal job then take another job in the meantime; it's easier to find work when you're already working.

GET THE BALANCE RIGHT

Work is an important part of life but it should never take over. Too many people have made the mistake of thinking that they must work extraordinarily long hours to be successful.

A recent report by the Institute of Management found that 87 percent of executives said that their work left them no time for other interests, including their partners and families. A third worked more than 50 hours a week, a tenth more than 60 hours and two-thirds felt constantly under pressure. As novelist Celia Brayfield points out: 'This is a way of life you could not offer a dog without risking a raid by animal rights activists.'

Money is important, but many people are simply earning lots of money in order to pay other people to run their lives and keep them at work. If you're paying people to clean your house, do your gardening, look after your children and walk your dog then it's time to think about how valuable your job really is to you.

By all means pay people to do things you don't want to do, but don't keep yourself from having a life by working crazy hours. Working excessively long hours on a continuous basis is actually a sign of failure. People who do this are usually avoiding other parts of their lives, rather than working creatively. To stay truly creative and to enjoy what you do it is important to define and stick to your working hours and to leave work behind when you finish for the day.

People who are genuinely successful, as opposed to simply making loads of money, go home and spend time with their families, go out and play, do things they love doing, take holidays, laugh and see friends.

EXERCISE

I want you to look at your life and the place work has in it. Be really honest and ask yourself these questions:

1) *Am I working too much or too little?*
2) *Do I earn plenty of money but feel unhappy and under pressure?*
3) *Do I need to earn more but have no idea how?*
4) *Is my home/work life out of balance?*
5) *Do I dread and resent going to work?*
6) *Do I feel trapped in my job because of my financial responsibilities?*

If you answered *yes* to even one of these questions then you need to review and reconsider your working life and to decide whether it's time to make changes.

WHAT DO YOU NEED TO CHANGE

Decide right now what it is about your work that needs changing. If you love what you do but work excessive hours or hate the company for which you work then you may need to leave.

If what you want is promotion or a pay rise then you need to get yourself noticed by the people who make these decisions. Develop a high profile, put extra effort into coming up with great ideas and make your contributions, both written and spoken, bright, to the point and effective. Do something different, like writing great articles for the in-house journal. One salesman I heard about recently was asked by the company chairman to write for the company magazine. The salesman asked a journalist friend to help him with his ideas and writing style. His work was so impressive that he was soon promoted and is now on the board of the company.

Making alterations to the way you work is always possible. And it may be that the changes you need to make are big rather than small. Is it time for a total career change – a switch from one working life to another? Many people who do this feel a new, lighter energy and feel years younger. More and more people are realising that you can have two or more entirely different careers and be successful in all of them. I recently met a man whose story is a perfect example of this.

HENRY'S STORY
HENRY HAD WORKED FOR TWENTY-SEVEN YEARS IN THE CITY OF LONDON AS AN INVESTMENT ANALYST AND BANKER, AND, MORE RECENTLY RUNNING HIS OWN PROPERTY INVESTMENT COMPANY. IT WAS ONLY WHEN A PERSISTENT BACK PROBLEM SENT HIM IN SEARCH OF A CURE THAT HE BEGAN TO QUESTION HIS CHOICE OF CAREER. AFTER ORTHODOX MEDICINE HAD FAILED TO HELP, HENRY, AT A

FRIEND'S SUGGESTION WENT TO SEE A TIBETAN MEDICAL PRACTITIONER. AS THE PHYSICIAN BEGAN TO WORK ON HIS BACK, HENRY BEGAN TO REVIEW HIS WHOLE LIFE.

'I REALISED HOW DEEPLY UNHAPPY AND UNSATISFIED I WAS IN MY JOB,' HE SAYS. 'IT WAS A SHOCK TO REALISE I HAD BEEN IN THE WRONG JOB FOR TWENTY-SEVEN YEARS. I WAS ALSO UNHAPPY IN MY TWELVE-YEAR RELATIONSHIP WITH MY GIRLFRIEND. I KNEW I'D HAVE TO MAKE CHANGES, BUT IT WAS A FRIGHTENING PROSPECT.'

THE CLEARER HENRY BECAME ABOUT THE NEED TO CHANGE HIS LIFE, THE MORE HIS BACK IMPROVED. 'I TOOK SOME TIME OFF WORK AND DURING THAT TIME I REALISED THAT I COULDN'T POSSIBLY GO BACK TO MY JOB,' HE SAYS. 'IT WAS A VERY DIFFICULT PERIOD. I EVEN HIT THE BOTTLE FOR A WHILE. BUT THE ONLY WAY FORWARD WAS TO LEAVE MY JOB AND TO END MY RELATIONSHIP. I DIDN'T KNOW WHAT I WAS GOING TO DO NEXT, BUT I KNEW I'D DONE THE RIGHT THING.'

WHEN YOU CLOSE A DOOR, ANOTHER ONE OPENS, AND THIS WAS ALMOST IMMEDIATELY TRUE FOR HENRY.

'I BECAME DEEPLY INTERESTED IN TIBETAN MEDICINE, WHICH HAD DONE SO MUCH FOR ME,' HE SAYS. 'I DECIDED TO SET UP A CLINIC, A CENTRE OF EXCELLENCE, FOR COMPLEMENTARY HEALTH PRACTITIONERS TO WORK ALONGSIDE ORTHODOX DOCTORS.' HENRY WENT AHEAD AND CREATED HIS DREAM. AT THE HUGELY SUCCESSFUL CLINIC HE SET UP IN LONDON, THE EDEN MEDICAL CENTRE, GPS WORK ALONGSIDE COMPLEMENTARY HEALERS OF ALL KINDS.

'I'M DOING SOMETHING I REALLY BELIEVE IN AND ENJOY,' SAYS HENRY. 'IT WAS VERY TOUGH MAKING THE BREAK, BUT IT WAS ALSO THE BEST THING I EVER DID.'

WHAT IS IT YOU WANT TO DO?

Before you can go for your ideal job you need to know what it is. Lots of my clients say that they're not happy in what they're doing but they don't know what else to do. I believe that every one of us knows what we want to do, but all too often we hide it away, deny it or consider it impossible.

Everyone has something they love doing – something they're really good at, which gives them enormous pleasure. For some it's a hobby, for others just a dream and for others it's buried so deep that they don't even know it's there until they start to dig deep inside themselves to uncover their talents and abilities.

Many people believe that they can't possibly earn a living doing something that they love. They separate work and pleasure in their minds, believing that work has to be dull and routine and that the things they enjoy doing can only be fitted in around work and other commitments.

ROBIN'S STORY

ROBIN WAS A VERY SUCCESSFUL AND HARD-WORKING COMPUTER EXPERT WHO CAME TO ME BECAUSE HE FELT STIFLED AND UNHAPPY IN HIS JOB. HE HAD WORKED FOR A TOP FIRM FOR FIFTEEN YEARS AND HE FELT TRAPPED BY HIS OWN SUCCESS. HOW COULD HE WALK AWAY FROM A JOB THAT SO MANY PEOPLE WOULD ENVY? FROM SUCH A GOOD INCOME? FROM THE PERKS AND ADVANTAGES HIS COMPANY OFFERED? WOULDN'T EVERYONE THINK HIM MAD?

I TOLD ROBIN THAT IT DIDN'T MATTER WHAT OTHER PEOPLE THOUGHT, OR WHO ELSE MIGHT ENVY HIS JOB. TO HIM IT WAS REPRESSIVE, BORING AND DULL AND ALL HE WOULD BE WALKING AWAY FROM WAS THE MISERY AND UNHAPPINESS OF BEING IN THE WRONG JOB.

ROBIN AGREED WITH ME, BUT HE STILL HAD NO IDEA WHAT HE WANTED TO DO. I ASKED HIM TO THINK ABOUT ALL THE THINGS HE WAS GOOD AT AND REALLY ENJOYED, WITHOUT WORRYING ABOUT WHETHER HE COULD EARN A LIVING DOING THEM OR NOT. HE CAME

BACK TO ME WITH A LIST. HE LOVED PAINTING, MUSIC, WALKING IN THE COUNTRY AND DANCING.

IT TURNED OUT THAT ROBIN WAS A TALENTED AMATEUR TANGO DANCER. HE WENT WITH HIS GIRLFRIEND TO CLASSES EVERY WEEK AND LOOKED FORWARD TO IT FOR THE WHOLE WEEK BEFORE EACH CLASS. WHY NOT OPEN A DANCE STUDIO? I SUGGESTED. ROBIN WAS STUNNED BY THE IDEA AND CAME UP WITH A DOZEN REASONS WHY IT COULDN'T POSSIBLY WORK. ONCE WE'D GONE THROUGH THEM AND HE REALISED NONE WERE REAL OBSTACLES HE BEGAN TO GET MORE AND MORE ENTHUSIASTIC ABOUT THE IDEA. A WEEK LATER ROBIN RESIGNED FROM HIS JOB AND BEGAN LOOKING FOR PREMISES FOR HIS STUDIO.

WITHIN TWO MONTHS HE'D FOUND THE RIGHT PLACE, RENOVATED AND DECORATED IT, HIRED A TEACHER AND STARTED ADVERTISING A WHOLE RANGE OF DANCE CLASSES.

A YEAR ON, ROBIN'S STUDIO IS A HUGE SUCCESS. HE'S GOT THE BEST TEACHERS AND THE HIPPEST STUDIO IN TOWN AND PEOPLE ARE FLOCKING THERE. ROBIN ISN'T EARNING THE SAME SALARY HE DID BEFORE, THOUGH HE PROBABLY WILL BE SOON. HE'S WORKING LONGER HOURS THAN HE DID BEFORE, OFTEN LATE INTO THE EVENING, BUT HE'S HAPPIER THAN HE'S EVER BEEN. HE LOVES WHAT HE DOES AND HE CAN'T WAIT TO GET TO WORK EVERY DAY.

'THIS DOESN'T FEEL LIKE WORK,' HE TOLD ME. 'I'M JUST HAVING A GREAT TIME AND GETTING PAID FOR IT.'

EXERCISE

Take your pen and paper and answer these statements, without thinking about jobs or work:

1) *Five talents I have are . . .*
2) *Five things I love doing are . . .*

3) *Five careers I wish I'd had are . . .*
4) *Five things people tell me I'm good at are . . .*
5) *Five things I'd love to try doing are . . .*

What emerged from this exercise? Are you beginning to see a pattern and to get a feel for what you're good at and love doing? What's fascinating is that for every person it's different. One person is great at talking, another is brilliant at doing up houses, a third loves travelling and being with other people. All of these talents can lead to a variety of jobs, from disc jockey (for the talker) to air steward (for the traveller) or interior designer (for the house decorator). There's no limit to the amount and variety of jobs in the world and I find it exciting and inspiring to see my clients discover their talents and begin to use them in their working lives.

At this point you may still be unclear about what exactly it is that you want to do. Perhaps the things you like doing and are good at don't seem to you like potential sources of income. If you've put down swimming, reading and watching TV then you may not be inspired yet, though even here there are lots of potential careers – a swimming instructor? manuscript editor? TV producer?

If you're not getting excited and finding all sorts of possibilities occurring to you then go back and think again about the lists you made in the above exercise. Is there something you've missed or dismissed as irrelevant? What would you love to try, if there were absolutely no obstacles in your way?

Let your imagination fly. Think of things you've read about and been inspired or moved by. Think of the last time you really enjoyed yourself. What were you doing?

BE WILLING TO LEARN

What hugely successful people have in common is their willingness to learn and to adapt or re-invent themselves. There are thousands of people successfully running their own businesses and making lots of money doing what they love. They are people who prize freedom, independence and the opportunity to make their own choices. They are people who never stop learning.

Look at those around you who are succeeding and learn from them. Notice what you do that works and what doesn't and listen to the advice of people you trust. Don't be afraid to go back to basics and learn new skills. If you want to set up in business then you may need to learn business skills, computer skills or some accountancy. If you want to be a chef, find a great chef who will let you into their kitchen to learn, and be willing to wash dishes when you start out.

Your dream job may involve a training period when you will be earning less. You need to be flexible and self-confident to do this, knowing that it's worthwhile because you'll achieve your goal.

MARY'S STORY

WHEN MARY FIRST CONTACTED ME SHE WAS THIRTY-SIX AND WORKING ON THE INFORMATION DESK AT LONDON'S HEATHROW AIRPORT. SHE WAS BORED WITH HER JOB AND LONGED FOR A CHANGE. AS WE TALKED IT BECAME CLEAR THAT MARY'S DREAM WAS TO BECOME A FLIGHT ATTENDANT. 'I SEE THEM WALK PAST ME EVERY DAY, HEADING FOR EXOTIC LOCATIONS, AND I WISH I COULD JOIN THEM,' SHE SAID. 'I WOULD LOVE TO TRAVEL AND I'M GREAT WITH PEOPLE. BUT I'M TOO OLD. ALL THE TRAINING PROGRAMMES ARE FULL OF GIRLS IN THEIR TWENTIES. THEY'D NEVER CONSIDER ME FOR THE JOB.'

I EXPLAINED TO MARY THAT IF SHE DIDN'T THINK SHE'D GET THE

JOB THEN ANY POTENTIAL EMPLOYERS WOULD PICK UP ON THIS AND INSTANTLY AGREE WITH HER. I ASKED HER INSTEAD TO LOOK AT ALL THE QUALITIES AND EXPERIENCE SHE COULD BRING TO THE JOB.

WE WORKED ON BUILDING HER SELF-ESTEEM AND BELIEF IN HERSELF AND MARY ALSO LOST WEIGHT, CHUCKED OUT HER FRUMPY CLOTHES AND HAD HER HAIR CUT IN A GREAT NEW STYLE.

THEN SHE APPLIED TO THE AIRLINE OF HER CHOICE FOR A FLIGHT ATTENDANT'S JOB. A FEW DAYS AFTER HER INTERVIEW SHE WAS THRILLED TO BE OFFERED THE JOB. THAT WAS A YEAR AGO AND MARY IS NOW WINGING HER WAY ALL OVER THE WORLD AND HAVING A FANTASTIC TIME.

BE YOUR OWN BOSS

Whatever it is that you decided you want to do I want to encourage you to do on your own time and in your own way – in other words by being your own boss and becoming self-employed. If you've spent years working for other people then this idea may seem frightening and horribly insecure. *What about my sick pay, holiday pay, job security, pension and promotion prospects?* you may wonder. But, in fact, the only true security in life comes when you depend on yourself, rather than on others. Many people who have stuck in dull jobs because of the supposed security they offer have been made redundant, sacked, made to move location or simply ended up miserable and depressed.

When you are self-employed you are in control of your life; you make your own decisions, work in the way you want to and take responsibility for your life. If something isn't working, you change it. You are in a position to dip constantly into your inner resources and come up with answers. Those who are successfully self-employed always have a high degree of self-worth and self-reliance. They have proven that they can trust and rely on themselves, motivate themselves and make the right choices about their working lives. You can do anything an employer would have done for you, including organising your own perks and benefits and adding a few more that you didn't have before, such as time off when you need it.

Look around at the people you know. Chances are those who like their work most are the ones who are working for themselves.

JULIA'S STORY

JULIA CAME TO ME BECAUSE SHE WANTED TO MAKE CHANGES TO HER WORKING LIFE. SHE WAS A SENIOR MEMBER OF THE HUMAN RESOURCES DEPARTMENT OF A LARGE COMPANY AND WAS WELL PAID. BUT SHE WAS WORKING A TWELVE HOUR DAY AND SHE FELT EXHAUSTED AND DRAINED. ON TOP OF THAT HER COMPANY HAD TOLD HER THAT IF SHE WANTED PROMOTION SHE WOULD HAVE TO MOVE TO ANOTHER TOWN, SOMETHING SHE WAS VERY RELUCTANT TO DO.

JULIA HAD STARTED OUT A FEW YEARS EARLIER LOVING HER JOB. BUT THE LONG HOURS, CONSTANT DEMANDS AND REPETITIVE ASPECTS OF HER JOB HAD LEFT HER DISILLUSIONED AND MISERABLE.

JULIA TOLD ME THAT SHE WANTED TO FIND A WAY TO WORK SHORTER HOURS. I ASKED HER WHY SHE WASN'T THINKING OF CHANGING HER CAREER TOTALLY, SINCE SHE CLEARLY NO LONGER LIKED WHAT SHE WAS DOING.

SHE WAS STUNNED AND TOLD ME SHE SIMPLY HADN'T THOUGHT OF THIS AS A POSSIBILITY. 'I LIKE MY SALARY AND ALL THE BENEFITS,' SHE TOLD ME. 'IT MEANS I CAN TAKE EXOTIC HOLIDAYS AND THAT'S WHAT KEEPS ME GOING.' I POINTED OUT THAT GETTING THROUGH LIFE BY HANGING ON FOR THE NEXT HOLIDAY WAS NOT A GREAT WAY TO LIVE AND ASKED HER TO IMAGINE ENJOYING ALL OF HER LIFE, NOT JUST THE PARTS WHEN SHE ESCAPED FROM WORK.

JULIA LOVED THE IDEA AND DECIDED THAT SHE WOULD RATHER ENJOY HER WORK AND HAVE FEWER HOLIDAYS, IF NECESSARY. WE BEGAN TO LOOK AT HER TALENTS AND ABILITIES. IT TURNED OUT THAT SHE HAD MOVED HOUSE SEVERAL TIMES AND EACH TIME SHE HAD ENJOYED DOING UP THE GARDENS OF HER HOMES, TRANSFORMING THEM FROM RUBBISH DUMPS INTO COLOURFUL, BEAUTIFUL RETREATS.

I SUGGESTED THAT SHE THINK ABOUT BECOMING A GARDEN DESIGNER, ADVERTISING HER SERVICES AND BUILDING UP EXPERIENCE AND A PORTFOLIO OF PICTURES BY WORKING ON HER FRIENDS' GARDENS. TWO MONTHS LATER, HAVING GOT HER FIRST GARDEN DESIGN COMMISSION, SHE RESIGNED FROM HER JOB AND LAUNCHED HER BUSINESS. THREE MONTHS AFTER SHE BEGAN SHE HAD AS MANY COMMISSIONS AS SHE COULD HANDLE AND TOLD ME SHE FELT FREED BY BEING SELF-EMPLOYED. 'I WORK VERY HARD,' SHE SAID, 'BUT I'M NOT DOING THE HOURS I DID IN MY PREVIOUS JOB. I GIVE MYSELF REGULAR TIME OFF AND, MOST IMPORTANTLY, I LOVE WHAT I DO.'

MAKING CHANGES
So now you've got an idea, or several about what you want. How are you going to go about making the necessary changes in your life? Here's my four-step plan for creating your ideal working life.

CHANGE YOUR MINDSET
Like Julia, you've got to believe it's possible before you begin to make changes. You've got to imagine yourself in your new job, see yourself making a success of it and think of yourself as someone who does that job.

Write a list of all your doubts, fears and negative thoughts around the idea of changing jobs. Then go through it, answering each point with a positive solution or affirmation. For instance, if you're telling yourself that you wont find people who want to use your services then answer this by pointing out that you are reliable, committed and willing to persevere until you get the clients you want. Not only this but you are full of creative ideas about ways to advertise your services and attract clients.

In *The Seven Spiritual Laws of Success,* the spiritual writer and teacher Deepak Chopra talks about the wisdom of uncertainty. You can seek a lifetime for security and not find it, he says, whereas if you are willing to live with uncertainty you will also allow in endless possibilities. Focus strongly on your talents, abilities and qualities and don't allow yourself to indulge in negative thinking that will hold you back.

BUILD A BRIDGE

Plan the route you take into your new job or business. Back up your determination and enthusiasm by being organised and thorough in the detailed planning. Look at the necessary steps, set a time limit for having everything in place and work out what you will need to do every day until then to make your plan work. For instance you may need to talk to your bank manager, organise an advertising campaign, contact people who can help and advise you and sort out where and how you will work.

Be open to every possibility and be creative in finding solutions. Don't allow yourself to be deflected or put off. Treat setbacks lightly and move on to the next potential solution or step forward.

Tell people who need to know or who can help you and keep quiet about your plans the rest of the time. Avoid telling anyone who might be discouraging or doubtful and if those close to you do behave in this way then detach yourself from their fears and stand firm in your own positive conviction. If you know, deep down, that you're doing the right thing then simply stick with it. Don't waste time trying to convince others, they will be convinced when they see you happy and successful in your new job.

JUMP

To move forward and allow new experiences, new energy and new people into your life you have to let go of whatever and whoever is not right for you anymore. Judge the right moment to leave your old job. You may need to leave and spend a few weeks recovering from the stress and misery before you have the energy to begin something fresh and new. If money is limited then you may want to do a transition job, like Emma (see page 68). Do something fun, something you've always fancied having a go at, like working in a shop or bar. See it as a recovery time and a way of earning some money and having fun while you prepare for the next stage. For the vast majority of people I work with, once the decision to make the change is taken they can't wait to get on with it. They leave their old jobs within a short period of time and move on to what they really want.

Sometimes this takes a great deal of courage, faith and self-reliance. It takes confidence in yourself and your abilities. This is where the self-worth and self-reliance you have created for yourself will really bring you rewards.

BRIAN'S STORY
BRIAN IS SOMEONE WHO SHOWED ENORMOUS SELF-RELIANCE WHEN HE DECIDED TO CHANGE HIS LIFE COMPLETELY — NOT JUST FOR HIMSELF BUT FOR HIS WIFE AND YOUNG FAMILY OF SIX CHILDREN AGED FROM TWO TO TWELVE. AT THE TIME THEY WERE LIVING IN AUSTRALIA, IN SYDNEY'S MOST EXCLUSIVE SUBURB, IN A SUMPTUOUS SIX-BEDROOM HOME COMPLETE WITH SWIMMING POOL. HIS CAREER WAS TREMENDOUSLY SUCCESSFUL AND, ONLY A FEW YEARS AFTER

EMIGRATING FROM NORTHERN IRELAND, BRIAN WAS AMONG THE TOP TWO PERCENT OF MANUFACTURING EXECUTIVES IN THE COUNTRY AND WAS ALSO THE YOUNGEST. IT WAS AT THIS POINT THAT BRIAN AND HIS WIFE DECIDED TO RETURN TO IRELAND TO MAKE A FRESH START. HIS COLLEAGUES AND FRIENDS THOUGHT HIM COMPLETELY MAD. THEY SUGGESTED HE TAKE SOME LEAVE AND RENT OUT HIS HOME SO THAT HE COULD RETURN IF IT DIDN'T WORK OUT. BUT BRIAN REFUSED.

'I KNEW I HAD TO BURN ALL MY BRIDGES IF I WAS REALLY GOING TO START ALL OVER AGAIN AND MAKE A GO OF IT,' HE TOLD ME. 'MAKING IT EASY TO RETURN WOULD HAVE WEAKENED MY RESOLVE AND BESIDES, I WAS CONFIDENT THAT I'D MAKE IT WORK.'

SO BRIAN BURNED HIS BRIDGES AND RETURNED TO A WARM WELCOME IN IRELAND WITH EIGHT MOUTHS TO FEED AND NO JOB. THE LIMITED AMOUNT OF SAVINGS HE HAD BEGAN TO DWINDLE FAST. BUT BRIAN NEVER REGRETTED HIS DECISION OR DOUBTED HIS ABILITY TO GET BACK ON TRACK. HE SIMPLY SAW HIMSELF AS THE SORT OF PERSON WHO WOULD ULTIMATELY WIN THROUGH.

BRIAN'S FAITH PAID OFF WHEN HE HAD A CALL FROM THE IRISH DEVELOPMENT AUTHORITY. THEY WANTED HIM TO MEET UP WITH A WEALTHY GERMAN INDUSTRIALIST WHO THEY WERE HOPING WOULD MAKE IRELAND HIS NEW EUROPEAN BASE. HE WAS UNIMPRESSED WITH ALL HE HAD SEEN SO FAR AND WAS PLANNING TO FLY HOME THE NEXT DAY. THE AGENCY HOPED THAT BRIAN COULD CHANGE HIS MIND.

BRIAN JOINED THE INDUSTRIALIST FOR DINNER, FLEW TO GERMANY WITH HIM THE NEXT DAY AND FORMED A PARTNERSHIP WITH HIM THAT WAS HUGELY SUCCESSFUL. SO SUDDEN WAS BRIAN'S SUCCESS THAT HIS BANK MANAGER CALLED TO ASK WHETHER THERE HAD BEEN AN ERROR WHEN HIS MODEST SAVINGS SWELLED TO A SIX-FIGURE SUM ALMOST OVERNIGHT.

NOW BRIAN HAS A STRING OF BUSINESSES, INCLUDING HIS OWN GOLF CLUB, WHICH THE IRISH PRIME MINISTER OPENED. WHAT BRIAN DID WAS TO TAKE ABSOLUTE RESPONSIBILITY FOR CREATING THE NEW LIFE THAT HE WANTED. HE ALSO MADE THE DECISION TO TRUST HIS INGENUITY, RESOURCEFULNESS, DETERMINATION AND SHEER GUTS. AND FINALLY HE CHOSE TO LISTEN TO HIMSELF WHEN EVERYONE AROUND HIM WAS ADVISING HIM AGAINST HIS COURSE OF ACTION. HE IGNORED ALL COUNSEL EXCEPT HIS OWN. AND AS A RESULT HIS FAITH IN HIMSELF AND HIS STOCK OF SELF-RELIANCE WERE CATAPULTED INTO ANOTHER LEAGUE. HE BECAME ONE OF THE ELITE RANKS OF INDIVIDUALS WHO TRUST AND RELY ON THEMSELVES AND AS A RESULT DISPLAY A DISTINCT PERSONAL POISE AND CHARISMA THAT MAKE THEM STAND OUT. BRIAN'S STORY IS A PARTICULARLY SPECIAL ONE TO ME BECAUSE HE'S SOMEONE TO WHOM I AM PARTICULARLY CLOSE. HE IS MY OLDER BROTHER.

KEEP ON TRACK

Once you've made your decision, put the steps in place and then jumped it's vital that you keep yourself on track towards your goal. Don't give up.

Many people have failed in new ventures simply because they weren't prepared to deal with the hurdles and to keep on going until they succeeded. So set yourself goals but not restrictions or time limits. Be determined and not defeatist. Go for it and keep on going with your end view clearly in sight all along the way.

You know what you want and there is nothing and no one – except yourself – to stop you from having it. Setbacks and disappointments are just a normal part of any venture, so take them in your stride and concentrate on your achievements and successes.

Learn from what you're doing; notice what works and what doesn't. Let go of anything that doesn't benefit you and your goals, and never let your dreams be diminished or diluted. You deserve the best and you're giving it to yourself.

If you are your own boss then be a good one. Encourage, reward, praise and value yourself if you expect to work hard and achieve great things. It takes grit and determination to create a new way of working for yourself and to make it succeed.

YOUR ASSIGNMENT

I want you to set up your own business. Yes, I said business! And I want you to do it now, beginning tonight. What kind of business? I can guarantee it's staring you in the face. Whatever your hobby is, whatever your interests, whatever you've always wanted to do but not got round to, now's the time to turn it into a thriving money-spinner.

I'm not insisting you give up your day job. Your new business is a sideline – for now. Everyone should know what it's like to have their own business, however small, and everyone should have a second string to their bow. It's great for your self-worth to know that you can do more than one thing and to have something to fall back on, should you need it. If you've already got a sideline or a second business then start another one! And get your kids doing it, too. Some kids are fantastically enterprising and run very successful business operations from their bedrooms, selling their paintings, models or outgrown toys. Encourage them to use their talents, interests and skills just as you are doing. Even if you only give your new business one evening a week, that's fine. You can make it as big or as small as you want it to be.

And if you're objecting because the hours you already work are too long then you more than anyone else need to make this change. You obviously haven't got enough to do with yourself if you can afford to devote all those hours to your job!

AND REMEMBER . . .
You can do any job you want to do.
> *The best boss to have is yourself.*
> *Self-employment means self-reliance and self-worth.*
> *True security comes from depending on yourself.*
> *Your ideal job is probably staring you in the face.*
> *Follow your heart — do work that you love.*

CHAPTER EIGHT

How Attractive Are You?
How To Be Gorgeous and Highly Desirable

IN THIS chapter I want to look at how attractive you think you are and how you imagine others see you. If you don't think you are attractive and don't feel confident about your looks then you're creating a major obstacle for yourself in your life. It's as important to feel confident, attractive and sure of yourself on the outside as it is to feel these things inside. So far we've concentrated on what's going on inside – your feelings about who you are and who you want to be. Now it's time to look at the outside and whether your opinion of your looks matches the dazzling sense of self-worth you've been working hard to develop.

I want you to grasp this elementary truth: you are as attractive as you consider yourself to be. I want you to feel equal to anyone else, to enjoy your own intrinsic magnetism and your special brand of gorgeousness so that you attract only confirmation of this from others around you. Other people will generally accept your estimation of yourself. I want to make sure it's a damn fine estimation.

Rebecca's story

Rebecca had been a client for six months when we decided to meet for lunch to celebrate the launch of her new mail-order fashion business. Our sessions had taken place over the phone, so we were meeting face to face for the first time.

As I entered the restaurant I spotted her immediately. At thirty-five she was tall and slim with the most fabulous lustrous blonde hair. She had piercing blue eyes and a perfect English rose complexion. She was, in short, gorgeous. Halfway into our lunch I found myself questioning my initial reaction. Was she really gorgeous or was she . . . ugly! I was especially perplexed to find myself thinking like this as ugly is just not a word I use in this way. Thinking it over on the train home the answer flashed before me. *I* didn't think Rebecca was ugly, but *she* did!

Thoughts have wings; you can't keep them to yourself. The more you think them and the stronger you feel about them, the more you project them outwards to others. I am schooled in identifying people's thoughts, so I am able to disentangle what I think and feel from other people's thoughts and feelings. With Rebecca I was picking up loud and clear her own belief that she was ugly.

Most people will not pick up and identify your thoughts as distinctly as I did with Rebecca. Instead, what will happen is that they will simply take on board whatever you are projecting as their own thoughts and then see you and treat you in the corresponding manner. This feeds back to you and confirms your own opinion of yourself, however warped.

Rebecca's personal issues had never been discussed during

OUR SESSIONS, AS WE HAD FOCUSED EXCLUSIVELY ON HER BUSINESS. AT OUR NEXT SESSION I CONFIDED MY OBSERVATIONS TO REBECCA AND INVITED HER RESPONSE. SHE IMMEDIATELY ADMITTED THAT THIS WAS PRECISELY HOW SHE SAW HERSELF AND HAD DONE ALL HER LIFE. SHE HAD NEVER ADMITTED THIS TO ANYONE ELSE, NOR HAD SHE RAISED THE MATTER WITH ME, AS SHE FELT UTTERLY RESIGNED TO FEELING THIS WAY ABOUT HERSELF.

HER SELF-LOATHING WAS SO SEVERE THAT THERE WERE DAYS WHEN SHE DIDN'T LEAVE THE HOUSE BECAUSE SHE FELT GROTESQUE AND FREAK-LIKE. SHE SPENT A FORTUNE ON BEAUTY TREATMENTS, WAS OBSESSED WITH HER WEIGHT AND WAS NOW CONSIDERING BREAST ENLARGEMENTS. HER MARRIAGE SUFFERED UNDER THE STRAIN AND, INEVITABLY, HER CHILDREN FELT HER TENSION AND UNHAPPINESS. AS A CHILD REBECCA HAD FELT SHE WAS A HUGE DISAPPOINTMENT TO HER FATHER, WHO HAD WANTED A BOY. SHE WAS NOT THE SPARKLING ACADEMIC HER SISTER WAS AND GREW UP WITH THE INTENSE FEELING THAT SHE WAS UGLY. THIS WAS THE PRECISE WORD SHE USED AND THE VERY ONE ONTO WHICH I HAD LATCHED. THE REALITY IS THAT SHE IS STUNNING, WITH CLASSIC COVER GIRL LOOKS. SHE'S ALSO ONE OF THE MOST INTERESTING AND ORIGINAL PEOPLE YOU COULD EVER MEET. WHAT A MONUMENTAL TRAGEDY FOR HER TO GO THROUGH LIFE NOT SEEING THIS.

REBECCA AGREED TO TACKLE THIS ISSUE WITH ME SO THAT SHE COULD BEGIN TO SEE HERSELF AS THE LOVELY WOMAN SHE ACTUALLY WAS. I BEGAN A PLAN OF ACTION TO TRANSFORM HER PERCEPTION OF HERSELF AND TO ERADICATE UGLINESS FROM HER THOUGHTS AND VOCABULARY.

YOU ARE AS ATTRACTIVE AS YOU THINK YOU ARE

The funny thing is that, on paper, Rebecca would be far more conventionally beautiful than me, yet she saw me as ten times more attractive than herself, pointing out how gorgeous, radiant and charismatic I was by comparison. What sort of thoughts and beliefs do you think I have consciously instilled in myself, to project outward to others? You got it!

I have chosen to see myself as gorgeous, radiant and charismatic. Rebecca fed back to me exactly what she *should* have, just as I had done with her. The loop was complete. Yet Rebecca is far more likely to end up on the cover of *Vogue* than I would ever be! I believe that I am about ten times more attractive than I might actually be. By dint of sheer conviction I have managed to convince many people of this. I admit I was extremely lucky to have a dad who adored me and I grew up expecting all other men to feel the same way! I have *never* felt that I wasn't good enough for any man. I have *never* seen any man – as beyond me or 'out of my league', in the way so many people do. It would just never, ever occur to me that someone would not find me attractive. This is a far easier way to go through life than Rebecca's, and it's the one I want for you.

If you've had a poor view of your attractiveness for some time it won't transform overnight. But if you approach what I'm going to share with you with an open mind then you can completely change the way you see yourself and therefore the way others see you. Remember when we looked at the role of your beliefs and expectations in Chapter five? Well what we're looking at here is the nature of your most private, personal beliefs about yourself. How you see yourself has a profound effect on how you present yourself to others, the way you carry yourself, the clothes you wear, the effort you put into looking your best. The better you feel you look the more effort you'll make over the way you look. Your entire demeanour will reflect the way you see yourself and cue others to respond accordingly.

Consider someone you regard as good-looking when you first meet but who, a few minutes later, seems a lot less attractive. This will be due to the simple truth that they don't see themselves in a good light. You are simply seeing them as they see themselves.

BE GORGEOUS

Being beautiful, pretty or handsome is pretty much dependent on your gene pool. The faces of Brad Pitt, Gwyneth Paltrow and Emmanuelle Beart are definitely works of fine art. No matter. If you're willing to do what it takes in the attitude department, along with a little exercise and the right grooming, you can be gorgeous, which is far, far more interesting, enduring and sexy than pretty or handsome.

Regular pretty or good-looking does not necessarily go hand in hand with drop-dead gorgeous or sexy. The great news is that being gorgeous is something you can, and in my opinion, must, cultivate. In the words of Nelson Mandela: 'Who are you to be brilliant, gorgeous, talented, fabulous? Actually, who are you not to be?'

WHAT IS GORGEOUS?

Gorgeous is sexy. Gorgeous is available to you for the asking. Gorgeousness is the essence of who you are and who you have designed yourself to be. It is far more than the shape of your face or the symmetry of your features; it involves your entire character. It's the sum total of everything you bring to the table. Gorgeous comes to those of us determined to acquire it, and remember, I'm including men in this as well.

I would argue that the primary entry requirement to this state of gorgeousness is to start believing you're gorgeous. You have to do everything in your power to convince yourself of this and to see yourself and treat yourself as gorgeous. Once you do this, you're on your way, because everyone else will follow your lead and also be convinced. In essence, you are gorgeous to the extent that you believe you are.

Exercise

Right now, ask yourself the following questions:

1) *How attractive do I think I am? Extremely, reasonably, not very or not at all?*
2) *Who have I decided is 'out of my league'? (Obviously if you're with a partner this question is for information only!)*
3) *Do I expect men/women to think of me as attractive and gorgeous?*

Don't do anything with this information for the moment. I just want to open these lines of enquiry at this stage.

Who is gorgeous?

Models and actresses often feel bad about their looks and consider themselves to be unattractive. Even Cindy Crawford, one of the world's top supermodels, admits that her public persona bears little resemblance to how she looks first thing in the morning. Her airbrushed image has more to do with two hours in hair and make-up, and photographic touch-ups than the gifts of nature. For the rest of us to see these finished images as real or to aspire to them is sheer folly.

Few British actresses conquer Hollywood in their early twenties and then go on to become one of the defining sex symbols of their generation. Julie Christie did so, yet she agonised over her appearance and felt herself to be ugly. During filming of *Darling*, which was to win her an Oscar and launch her Hollywood career, she confided to director John Schlesinger that she didn't want to play a nude scene as she didn't feel beautiful enough. She told him: 'I will be unattractive to people.' Astonishing but true. This luminously beautiful 24-year-old, seen by many as Britain's answer to Brigitte Bardot, was convinced that her looks would make cinema-goers turn away in disgust. This entirely proves the point that it is up to us to decide how we see ourselves.

Conventional beauty, such as that which Julie Christie undoubtedly possesses, does not automatically mean that you see yourself as attractive or that you imagine others will find you attractive either. At the same time, Hollywood is full of men and women who have made their mark on the world by convincing us of their sex appeal, even though they have none of the God-given beauty of a Julie Christie.

Take Sophia Loren, who was recently voted the world's most beautiful woman by a men's magazine, despite the fact that she is sixty-six this year. Sophia's individual features: the large mouth, slightly bulging eyes, large nose and weak chin do not spell beauty, but Sophia Loren the package still projects a powerful sexual mystique which has maintained international appeal over four decades. The secret of her appeal must be, in part, her sheer gutsiness and personal power. She has lost none of the fiery determination she displayed at the start of her career when, as a sixteen-year-old, she ignored Hollywood bosses who told her that her nose was too big and her mouth too wide and that she should have plastic surgery.

'I've never hidden my age from the world because I don't care,' she says. 'Actually, I rather like birthdays. It's a good reason to talk to yourself, to ask yourself what you've been doing, what you are doing and what you will do. Girls who can't go off and talk to themselves stay girls and never become women. Women who can't take stock turn to drink, pills or worse, but I can take stock. I can send for the bill of life and add it up, too . . . it's not luck, I don't believe in luck, it's wanting that counts. I have always wanted. That is the secret of me . . . I wanted and I got. I did not want – ever – for others to get for me.'

Diana, Princess of Wales, was undoubtedly the most adored woman of our times. We adored her spirit, her compassion and her vulnerability. We perceived her as beautiful even though she had far from perfect features. We changed our take on beauty to accommodate her looks because she deserved it. Her character won through, and as she triumphed over her own self-loathing and her eating disorders, and developed self-respect and self-acceptance, so she became increasingly radiant and grew into one of the most charismatic women in the world. By the time of her death she had conquered her demons and grown into a dynamic, majestic and truly gorgeous human being.

Look at other gorgeous people in the public eye. Jack Nicholson is hardly good-looking, yet he oozes self-confidence and wicked sex appeal and has girls a quarter of his age falling over him, as does Gerard Depardieu, whose chunky, uneven looks are a world away from the stuff of classic leading men. Bob Hoskins is short and balding – and deeply sexy with it.

Oprah Winfrey, at any weight, is gorgeous. She exudes confidence, warmth and humour. Patti Smith spends most of her time looking as though she's just got out of bed, yet she has attracted some of the world's sexiest men. Chrissie Hynde, Courtney Love (before her plastic surgery) and Susan Sarandon are the same. None of them stack up as conventional beauties, yet they appear utterly gorgeous and they know it. In Britain look at Zoë Ball and Geri Halliwell. Neither is particularly pretty, let alone beautiful, yet they exude sex appeal and charisma. Think of people you know who are terrifically attractive to others and yet who wouldn't necessarily win a Miss World or Mr Universe pageant. Think of women you know who have no problem whatsoever attracting men and men who effortlessly draw women to them.

The point of all this is that the truly gorgeous people are the ones who act, appear and see themselves as gorgeous, no matter what their looks, shape or age.

WHO IS UGLY?

I have been around models who are held up as great beauties, yet their characters are anything but. I remember one in particular who used to attend the same gym as I did in London. She was well known for her appalling temper and obnoxious manner and staff ran for cover when she was around. One occasion I will never forget was during the heyday of 'Step' classes, when the classes had become so popular that you had to book your place. Just as our class was about to begin the said model, who we'll call Sarah, appeared and took up a space where clearly there wasn't really a space. The teacher asked her to leave, pointing out that the class was absolutely full. Sarah protested that she had been sold a ticket and had no intention of leaving. Clearly there had been a mistake and she should never have been sold the ticket. But Sarah was having none of it. She dug in and refused to budge, while twenty-seven of us watched in astonishment. Eventually another member volunteered to leave so that the class could continue, but the atmosphere was poisoned.

When I looked into the face of this young woman I didn't see the ravishing beauty who gazed out at me from magazine covers. I saw an ugly person, without a shred of warmth, humanity or gorgeousness. She was simply a deeply unpleasant human being, mean-spirited and obsessed only with her own needs and wants. This is the kind of person who is ugly, rather than someone with a particular set of physical characteristics.

The tragedy is that so many people believe they are ugly when they're clearly not. And, as comedienne Joan Rivers said: 'The psychic scars caused by believing that you are ugly leave a permanent mark on your personality.'

So please do me a favour and understand that ugly and gorgeous run deeper that you have been taught to believe. There are only ever gorgeous people or ugly people, never gorgeous or ugly faces. All the time you are moving in one direction or the other. Make sure you grasp the distinction and position yourself firmly on the road to gorgeousness.

GORGEOUS PEOPLE

Hugo is someone who effortlessly grasped what it takes to be gorgeous. At thirty-two he was at least 12 kg overweight, bit his fingernails to the quick and hadn't seen the inside of a gym since schooldays. He was no Hugh Grant matinee idol, yet he was one of the most sensationally attractive and charismatic men I had ever come across.

He was engaging and popular with men and women alike and the most socially adept individual I had ever seen. His job in the music business brought him into contact with some of the world's most famous pop stars and he was completely himself with them – as comfortable around them as he was with anyone else. He was equal to anyone and treated everyone in the same way. He was always invited to London's best parties and weddings and many stars considered him a close personal friend. He was adorable to women and never had a problem attracting terrific girlfriends, yet he was the least conceited person you could meet. He was entirely and intrinsically comfortable with himself – not when he had lost weight, given up smoking or stopped biting his nails, but right now, exactly as he was. Hugo was totally gorgeous, yet he had never trained himself to be or given it a moment's thought, he just *was*.

Of course there's always a reason why. You don't get to be that effortlessly attractive without good reason. And this is the reason: Hugo had received a gift from his parents that very few of us were lucky enough to be given. The gift he had from both parents was their unconditional love. He had been cherished and adored from the outset for the person that he was, not for who he might be or who they wanted him to be. Their total, all-embracing love was given with no strings or conditions attached. Even though his father was a highly important military figure in the British Intelligence Service, Hugo was never pressured to follow these impressive footsteps. When his musical talent became apparent at a very early age, his parents were both happy for him to follow his own path, a long way from a glittering military or diplomatic career. When he decided against pursuing a full-time career as a musician, despite his prodigious talent, that too was absolutely fine.

This unequivocal acceptance set him on a path of freedom from the insecurities and doubts that dog many people, including the God-given beautiful. Self-loathing or a craving to be liked and accepted was never going to figure in Hugo's script. Hugo simply expects to be liked and his good nature and humour are always enthusiastically received.

Heather Mills is another truly gorgeous person. At the age of twenty-seven she had it all – an exciting new boyfriend, a modelling career that was just taking off and a glamorous London life. Then, one day in August 1993, she was out shopping in Kensington High Street, London. She took two steps off the pavement – into the path of a police motorcyclist. Doctors were forced to amputate the lower half of her left leg.

In hospital Heather received a visit from the hospital counsellor, who told her bluntly: 'You must accept that men will not be attracted to you.'

This heartless remark might well have devastated her, but Heather replied: 'Listen, darling, if all my arms and legs were missing I'd still be a lot more attractive than you.' Go girl!

Since then she has made a career out of proving that counsellor wrong. She has challenged popular perceptions of disabled people by posing seductively in sexy underwear, had a string of eligible lovers and is currently the new love of Sir Paul McCartney. More than this, she has used her new-found fame to raise hundreds of thousands of pounds for landmine victims across the world in war zones such as Bosnia and Kosovo. Heather Mills could only ever be gorgeous and her model looks are only a part of the picture, along with her vitality, inner resolve and sheer muscle.

How do you limit your attractiveness?

If we accept that you are training everyone else how to see and treat you then we have to find out what sort of instructions, cues and messages you are sending out to others. I've worked with some very attractive people who send out lousy messages about their perceived level of attractiveness and how they think others will see them.

Exercise

To root out any lousy beliefs you might be harbouring, take five minutes to complete this exercise. As always, finish these statements with the first response that comes to mind. Don't worry about repeating yourself, just do it!

1) *My most negative thought about my looks is* . . .
2) *Another negative thought I have about my looks is* . . . (repeat five times)

3) *Above all, the most negative thought I have about my looks is . . .*
4) *Something I learned from my mother/father about my looks is . . .*
5) *Something else I learned from my mother/father about my looks is . . . (repeat five times and feel free to do this one separately for each parent if they gave you different messages)*
6) *Above all the main thing I learned from my mother/father about my looks is . . .*
7) *The main message I project to others about my looks is . . .*
8) *What I expect men/women (delete as appropriate) to think of my looks is . . .*
9) *The ways in which this holds me back are . . . (list five)*

We should have rooted out all of your unproductive thoughts and beliefs here. Remember, these are merely emotional habits, even if it feels as though you've had them forever. They may be so familiar that they feel as though they're part of you. They're not, but we may have to unglue them from you, if you're so closely attached to them that you have come to believe they are true. They'll only be true if you continue to feed them and choose to continue believing in them.

I appreciate that these beliefs and self-concepts are deeply personal and private. You may never have admitted them to anyone else before now. Well done for uprooting them here. We will apply the same methods as we have before in order to eradicate these beliefs and to replace them with productive alternatives that bring you far better results.

A remarkably common deep-seated thought I've come across with both men and women is that they see themselves as . . . fat and ugly! And this includes many glamorous figures, whom you might assume would be entirely happy with their appearance.

Let's work with this thought, and the others you came up with and turn them around:

- *I no longer need to believe I am fat or ugly.*
- *I no longer need to believe my mother's/father's thoughts about me.*
- *I am completely free of my mother's/father's thoughts about me.*
- *I now appreciate my natural beauty and attractiveness.*
- *I am wonderful just as I am.*
- *I like myself.*
- *I love and approve of myself.*
- *I now choose to appreciate myself exactly as I am.*
- *I now radiate vitality.*
- *I approve of myself completely, especially in the presence of men/women.*
- *I approve of my body completely, especially in the presence of men/ women/my partner/specific name.*
- *I am always relaxed and at peace, poised and serene.*

Choose three of these replacement beliefs with which to start working. Change them or add to them in any way that makes them more personal or powerful for you. Begin today and in thirty days you will have travelled a long way towards taking *these* beliefs on board as true and accurate. Write them down at least ten times first thing in the morning and ten times last thing at night, when your subconscious is most receptive to programming.

Say them to yourself repeatedly throughout the day as repetition is the key to programming the way you see yourself and what you believe to be true about your looks. Occasionally, writing or saying them to yourself might not be enough. You absorbed these unproductive beliefs by being told them repeatedly by an authority figure and/or repeating them to yourself. We must use the same highly effective method to replace them. It worked before and it will work now. Your future depends on your conscious thoughts.

As you begin to discipline your mind, your new conscious thoughts create new subconscious programmes. In the same way you can develop subconscious programming to drive a car, you can develop subconscious programming to be more successful and to see yourself as attractive. But it takes disciplined thinking and some time. Being positive for one day won't do. Strengthening your mind is like strengthening your body. If you do twenty push-ups and then race over to the mirror you wont see any difference. Similarly, if you think positive for twenty-four hours you will see little difference. But discipline your thinking for a few months and you will see bigger changes in your life than you will ever see in the gym.

I put it to you that your level of attractiveness and the extent to which others see you as attractive is a reflection of your most common conscious thoughts. Clean up your thinking and you'll begin to see yourself in a whole new way. The rule is: to be gorgeous you must convince yourself that you are. You *must* believe that you are. As Northern Ireland's top, never beaten salesman, my Dad used to say: 'You can only sell what you believe in.' So get yourself as convinced as you possibly can, be enthusiastic and passionate and then, only then, can you go out to sell it to others. *Convince yourself first*, was his number one rule and he was the best.

The reality that you experience in your life is comprised of whatever thoughts, beliefs and opinions you impress on your subconscious mind. Your subconscious cannot argue. It acts only from what you feed it, from the instructions you give it. And so your thoughts become your experiences. Remember, you have the capacity to choose those thoughts. Choose well. Choose to believe in your own intrinsic beauty, attractiveness and gorgeousness. Let yourself shine and get ready for others to admire your glow.

A good way of gauging your progress is to listen to the feedback of those around you. The more intensely you feel the new truth, the more strongly you will radiate it outwards and the quicker you will experience a response. Listen out for others using the very words that you are affirming to yourself.

I asked Tessa, a client, to do this and within a week of affirming her gorgeousness she began to get comments about how gorgeous she was from a boyfriend who had never commented on her looks before! Be diligent in your application, do the homework and I promise you'll get results. They may be gradual, but keep with it and one day you'll suddenly notice how far you've travelled. You'll have turned into the gorgeous creature that you were all along.

THE INFALLIBLE STRATEGY TO UPGRADE YOUR PAQ

Here is my foolproof, personally guaranteed strategy to upgrade your PAQ – Personal Attractiveness Quotient – to turbo-charged levels.

STEP ONE – SEE YOURSELF AS GORGEOUS

You have to do *everything in your power* to convince yourself that you are gorgeous before anyone else will be sold on it. The place to start is not on the outside – that comes a little later – but in the inside.

Ask yourself right now: 'How do I want others to see me?' and then decide to see yourself in this way. Put the words or phrases into the form of a productive statement of intent and *affirm it fanatically*. A simple example is: 'I see myself as gorgeous and so does everyone else'.

The funny thing is, the more you can see yourself as attractive the better looking you'll actually get! I have clients who report on this all the time. One in particular, Monica, now receives comments from men and women, who gush about how much younger, slimmer and more attractive she is now than years ago. One friend she hadn't seen for two years felt she had turned the clock back ten years! Admittedly she had lost a little weight, but the big change had really been that she had increased her PAQ by about three hundred percent. That shift had prompted her to pay attention to her grooming and appearance, but Monica glowed from the inside; the lipstick was merely the icing.

As a clever friend of mine once said: 'You wouldn't paint on a dirty wall!' You've got to give yourself a good scrubbing on the inside so that you polish up really well on the outside.

STEP TWO – BE A GORGEOUS PERSON

Remember: there are no ugly faces, only ugly people. Grasp this law and you're well on your way to doubling your gorgeousness overnight. Train yourself to look at people in this way and you'll start to see beauty and attractiveness in a deeper light. Because we've all been conditioned to see beauty in the shape of cosmetic, air-brushed images, we have to consciously expand our field of vision to include a far wider and deeper perception of beauty and attractiveness.

Decide which qualities you judge to be outstanding, make a list and commit to bringing more of these qualities into your own character. Look around at others who appear gorgeous in the widest sense. Ask yourself what it is about these people that draws others to them and impresses you. Then model yourself on these individuals and cultivate the same virtues for yourself.

Remember Hugo, who is gorgeous because of who he is? His particular brand of gorgeousness includes lightness, humour, generosity, humility and an unaffected and genuine liking and respect for others. He has the knack of making others feel appreciated and valued and, therefore, good about themselves.

All of Hugo's qualities are worth having, but this is the real essence of his gorgeousness and the reason he is magnetically attractive. Cultivate this single quality and you'll notice the difference in a week. Or, if you're great at it, in a day. To do it well you have to mean it. Forget shallow flattery, which will only make others flinch. Train yourself to see others' qualities and strengths and then feed what you notice back to them in an appropriate manner. Make a habit of doing this every day and it will become automatic. The difference this makes to other people is phenomenal. You'll notice them glow as it feeds their positive sense of who they are.

Make sure you offer these positive strokes as a gift. Don't do it expecting something in return. What you'll get back is a great feeling, as you see their response, and a chance to hone and refine who you are. As you increase your compassion you get to raise your own personal vibration, – your energy field – which you may know as your aura. This is an intrinsic step on your journey to true, captivating, deep gorgeousness.

It's a tremendous feeling to have your qualities recognised and appreciated by someone else, who really 'gets' who you are. When I do this with my clients it often comes as a huge shock if they've received very little of this acknowledgement from anyone else.

Think of some of the most compassionate human beings on the planet: the Dalai Lama radiates and captivates all who see him; his charisma can fill a stadium. Indian spiritual figures such as Sai Baba and Mother Meera are said to be similarly charismatic.

STEP THREE – BE GORGEOUS ON THE OUTSIDE
Once you've done the work on the inside it's time to look at how you're presenting yourself on the outside. Looking your best and

making the best of yourself are the objectives here. The more you think of yourself, the more you value your own worth, and the more effort you are likely to put into your personal appearance. And, of course, by doing this, you're sending out the message, loud and clear, that you take a pride in your physical appearance because you're worth it!

People – most often women – who don't put time, money and effort into grooming themselves are often martyrs and complete bores, attending to everyone else's needs above and beyond their own. The same people run themselves into the ground volunteering to take care of everyone else, baking cakes for school fêtes, camping with the Scouts, anything but taking some quality time to take a look at honouring themselves with a bit of TLC.

I came across a woman recently who was a perfect example of this kind of behaviour. She always put her husband and her sons before her, running herself ragged attending to their needs. She was permanently frazzled and exhausted because she volunteered for everything, despite having a job. I pointed out to her that her behaviour wasn't helping anyone. She was, in effect, teaching her sons that she didn't matter; she was passing on a message that she obviously believed about herself. If this sounds familiar, stop it immediately.

You don't have to be the village dogsbody to justify your existence. Relax, draw breath and take a look at yourself. When was the last time you had a fabulous haircut, facial, manicure, seaweed mud wrap, shiatsu, hot oil body treatment or whatever constitutes grooming and a bit of indulgence to you? Unless you shine and glow on the outside you're undervaluing your own personal worth and letting others see this too. What you're actually conveying is that you don't matter *that* much. So, make sure that you're at least covering the basics. Get the sharpest haircut you can afford. Never colour your hair yourself, always have it done by a professional. If you're unhappy with your body, do something about it once and for all. You have a choice. You can either decide to be completely happy with how it is or you can change it. If you decide to do this and you can afford it, consider hiring a great personal trainer and use them intensively for six weeks. Then you can ease off, as you'll be up and running, so to speak! Once you see some progress it's so much easier to keep up the momentum. See yourself as someone who loves to exercise and soon you will be.

Only ever wear clothes that you love. You'll give far more positive vibes about yourself when you do. Get into the habit of checking your clothes before you put them on. Never wear something just because it's comfortable. Make sure you're comfortable with your reflection first and foremost. Don't even wear 'degrading' clothes in private. Why? Because you're upgrading the way *you* see yourself, so *you* will be looking at yourself, even if no one else is.

VANESSA'S STORY

I ENFORCED THIS RULE WITH A CLIENT, VANESSA, WHO WANTED TO SEE HERSELF AS FAR MORE STYLISH AND SEXY THAN EVER BEFORE. SHE REVEALED THAT HER WARDROBE CONTAINED VERY FEW CLOTHES THAT WERE EITHER. OUT WENT MOST OF HER SLOPPY 'COMFORTABLE' TRACKSUIT BOTTOMS AND IN CAME A WHOLE NEW REPERTOIRE WITH WHICH SHE NEEDED TO GET COMFORTABLE AND WHICH ALLOWED HER TO SEE HERSELF IN A NEW AND IMPROVED LIGHT. HER SARTORIAL MODEL WAS THE GAMINE AUDREY HEPBURN – STYLISH, UNDERSTATED GLAMOUR. VANESSA WENT OUT AND BOUGHT HERSELF GORGEOUS CAPRI PANTS, KITTEN HEELS AND CHIC LITTLE TWINSETS.

SHE HAD TO TRAIN HERSELF TO GET SO COMFORTABLE WITH THIS

NEW LOOK THAT SOON IT APPEARED EFFORTLESS AND ENTIRELY IN KEEPING WITH WHO SHE WAS. THAT MEANT KEEPING IT UP AT ALL TIMES. FOR THE FIRST FEW MONTHS I REFUSED EVEN TO LET HER DO THE GARDENING IN SLOPPY CLOTHES; STYLISH AND SEXY DESIGNER JEANS WERE AS TATTY AS SHE WAS ALLOWED TO GET.

EFFORTLESS CHIC IS ANYTHING BUT. IT TOOK ABOUT THREE MONTHS FOR THIS TO WORK, BUT IT WAS WORTH IT. THE BIGGEST BONUS WAS THAT SHE TRANSFORMED HER VIEW OF HERSELF COMPLETELY. VANESSA BEGAN TO SEE HERSELF AS THE GORGEOUS, SEXY, BEAUTIFULLY DRESSED WOMAN SHE HAD BECOME.

STEP FOUR – EXUDE CONFIDENCE

Beauty counts. And it's no good pretending that it doesn't. Confidence counts as well – big time. It's confidence that puts a new complexion on what's attractive. Psychologist Oliver James, author of *Britain on the Couch,* says: 'Research shows that about 80 percent of women are not happy with the way they look, so that leaves only 20 percent who are. I suspect that that 20 percent are not the prettiest, by any means. The characteristics they probably do share are a positive sense of wellbeing and a strong feeling that they're glad to be them. From a man's point of view, if a woman is really being herself, radiates authenticity and has tangible self-esteem, even if she isn't stunning or doesn't have a great figure, it's likely that she will be perceived as extremely sexy.'

The same is true, of course, of men. Women are attracted to men who feel good about themselves, no matter what shape they are or how much hair they have. The evidence that confidence is a powerful ingredient of attractiveness was borne out by a recent research project carried out by Dr Nichola Rumsey of the University of the West of England.

The research team hired an actress to pose as a market researcher.

At various times she had a large 'port wine' stain painted on her face. She also varied the degree of confidence she put across. 'What we found was that the most favourable impressions were formed of the actress when she had a disfigurement, but also had high social skills,' says Dr Rumsey. 'We found it was her different levels of confidence that had polarised the view people had formed about her and her appearance.'

James Partridge, who was badly burned in a car accident, now runs a charity called 'Changing Faces' which helps people to cope with and feel confident about disfigurement. James says: 'When I was going through lots of plastic surgery I suddenly realised it wasn't the presentability of my face that was really going to count, it was the way I carried it. If I helped other people deal with me, then I didn't need to go on and on having surgery. Now I value my uniqueness. We are all unique and I happen to stand out a bit more . . . that gives me a lot of self-esteem. I know I feel good about myself inside and I reckon that I radiate that.'

So forget about trying to look perfect. Putting energy into becoming more confident, relaxed, interesting and amusing is a far surer route to greater attractiveness. The French call it 'being comfortable in your own skins'.

No discussion on looks or confidence would be complete without mentioning cosmetic surgery. The most frequently cited reason for having cosmetic surgery is to gain more confidence. Cosmetic surgery can sometimes help, but it won't necessarily do the trick. 'Last year I had a nose job,' says Tania, who is eighteen. 'It hasn't changed my life, except that I used to look at people with small noses and envy them and now I look at people with big noses and envy their confidence.'

Most people who feel good in their own skin, even those who are pressured by film studios or publicists, refuse to change the shape of their faces and they flourish because of, not in spite of, their so-called defects. How? Their unbeatable confidence, of course.

STEP FIVE — MAKE YOURSELF HAPPY

I've said it before and I'll say it one more time: you came into this world alone and you'll leave it alone, so please look after yourself well. The more responsibility you take for looking after yourself and providing for yourself, the more attractive you'll be to others.

Let me explain. There is absolutely nothing more *unattractive* than desperation. Neurotic neediness, in both men and women, is deeply distasteful and off-putting. Keep yourself a little mysterious and therefore far more desirable. The more you stay in-control, the more chance you have of long-term happiness. Let others see that there is more to you than meets the eye; exactly what that is, is *your* business.

Keep more of you to yourself. If others choose to spill their entrails all over the dinner table, that's fine. That's their prerogative. *You* do not follow suit. Under no circumstances feel obliged to match their confession, no matter how many tequila slammers you've just shared. You'll only regret it in the morning. Reveal only what you're really comfortable letting them see. Especially if your relationship is professional, when you run the risk of revealing information or views that others may not warm to in the clear light of day.

DAVID'S STORY

DAVID WAS A CLIENT WHOM I INTRODUCED TO A NUMBER OF TELEVISION PRODUCERS, AS HIS GOAL WAS TO MOVE INTO TELEVISION PRESENTING. WE HAD A TERRIFIC LUNCH AND ALL WAS GOING SWIMMINGLY, WITH EVERYONE AGREEING THAT DAVID WAS

UNDOUBTEDLY 'MADE FOR TELEVISION' AND PROMISING TO DO THEIR UTMOST TO ASSIST HIM.

WE ALL WENT OUR SEPARATE WAYS AND DAVID GAVE ONE OF THE PRODUCERS, JANE, A LIFT HOME. WHEN I SPOKE TO JANE THE NEXT DAY, HER OPINION OF DAVID HAD CHANGED COMPLETELY. SHE HAD LOST ALL INTEREST IN HELPING HIM AND HAD DECIDED SHE DIDN'T LIKE HIM THAT MUCH AFTER ALL. IT WAS A COMPLETE 180– DEGREE TURNAROUND FROM THE PREVIOUS DAY. IN FACT, SHE WENT ON, SHE FOUND HIM 'REALLY QUITE AN UNATTRACTIVE PERSON'.

I WAS BAFFLED AND RANG DAVID IMMEDIATELY TO FIND OUT WHAT HAD HAPPENED ON THE JOURNEY HOME. THIS IS WHAT HAD HAPPENED. IT WAS A LONG JOURNEY AND JANE HAD SPOKEN AT LENGTH ABOUT DEEPLY PERSONAL ISSUES AND RELATIONSHIPS. FINE, HER CHOICE. THE MISTAKE DAVID HAD MADE WAS IN RECIPROCATING, MATCHING HER REVELATION FOR REVELATION. UNFORTUNATELY NOT EVERYTHING DAVID SHARED MET WITH JANE'S APPROVAL AND CONCURRED WITH HER PERSPECTIVE AND SHE IMMEDIATELY SAW DAVID IN A DIFFERENT LIGHT. DAVID THOUGHT HE HAD BEEN FRIENDLY. HE HADN'T; HE'D BEEN INDISCREET, WHICH IS QUITE DIFFERENT, AND IN THIS CASE IT ALMOST BLEW HIS CHANCES OF GETTING INTO THE CAREER HE LONGED FOR.

Hold back and cultivate more self-containment. Constant craving, whether to be liked, loved, accepted or approved of by others, will eat away at your centre, your personal power, your very soul. And gorgeousness, attractiveness and charisma cannot flourish under these conditions. The only answer is to take better care of yourself, so that less of your needs are on show. Cherish yourself, so that you are already loved, valued and respected. And, above all, dont crave anyone so much that you trick yourself into thinking that you won't survive without them. You will. Remember, the challenge is to build sufficient confidence not to care whether people take you seriously or not, or find you attractive. Instead, it is to build some depth to your character and to live with your own respect and approval. And the by-product? You're a vastly more attractive, intriguing and interesting person as a result. Well done.

YOUR ASSIGNMENT

I want you to do two things to round off your quest for gorgeousness. Firstly, I want you to ask yourself how someone looking at you now would know that you prized yourself and considered yourself gorgeous. What do you need to add, alter or attend to? Whatever it is I want you to pick up the phone and book an appointment *right now*. Call the sharpest hairdresser you can afford, book a massage, a manicure or a session with a personal trainer. Secondly, I want you to *act as if*. Let me explain what I mean by telling you a story.

I was in a café one day when I spotted the most divine man a few tables away. I was about to make eye contact with him when I remembered that I hadn't got any make-up on and I wasn't dressed up. So I decided to try an experiment. I *pretended* that I was wearing my sexiest dress and my most glamorous make-up. I gave myself extra confidence by telling myself that I looked fantastic and then I caught his eye and smiled.

His response was exactly the one I wanted and what I would have expected if I'd been looking stunning. He smiled back and we spent a delicious few minutes flirting like crazy. I want you to do exactly the same, only I want you to do it for a week. I want you to pretend that you are the most gorgeous being who attracts men/ women wherever you go. Do this and I *promise* you will notice the difference. In fact, you will undoubtedly decide to carry on for the rest of your life.

AND REMEMBER . . .

Choose to be a gorgeous person right now.
  You are as attractive as you think you are.
  Act gorgeous and you'll start to feel gorgeous.
  Treat yourself as gorgeous and others will follow your lead.
  Always make the effort to look great.
  Confidence is sexy.
  Gorgeous people make others feel valued and Gorgeous.

CHAPTER NINE

LOOK AND FEEL FABULOUS FOREVER

HOW OLD do you feel, right at this moment? Older than your actual age? Round about the age you are? Or years younger? Did you leap out of bed this morning looking forward to your day and with the energy to do anything you want to do? Or did you drag yourself up, groaning that you felt tired and wishing you could stay where you were?

The answers to these questions are crucial, because there's no way you're going to have the fantastic life I want for you and you want for yourself, if your health and energy levels are low. People with low energy struggle along on a near-empty tank, simply getting by with the basics in life. They don't have the motivation or the stamina for more. That's not going to be you. To live an exciting life, to achieve your goals and to do whatever you want in life with enthusiasm and commitment you need bags of energy and peak-condition health.

That's what I'm going to help you to achieve in this chapter. You know, already, that I want the best for you and I want you to be the best. Well, that includes being in the best of health, having

energy levels that astonish everyone around you and knocking
years off your age. I want you to look and feel marvellous and to
know exactly how to keep yourself in great condition.

HOW OLD DO YOU WANT TO BE?

Why settle for growing old when you don't have to? Why
announce your age to the world when you can choose to be
any age you like? Age has never been so fluid and people have
never lived as long as they do now. A century ago old age had set in
by the age of forty. Only one in ten people lived to the age of sixty-
five. Today forty is young and a forty-year-old can expect to live at
least another forty or fifty years. Middle-aged has become an
outdated and taboo term. Now we have middle-youth. The stage
from thirty-five to fifty, when life used to be downhill all the way,
is now one of the richest, most exciting stages of life. Do you think
the likes of Twiggy, fifty, Lulu, fifty, Carol Vorderman, thirty-nine
or Michelle Collins, thirty-six, think of themselves as middle-aged?
Do you think Madonna, forty-one or Jerry Hall, forty-three
consider themselves past *anything*?

Have Sting, forty-seven, Mick Jagger, fifty-five, Tom Jones,
sixty or Rod Steward, fifty-five, swapped partying for a cardie and
slippers? I think not. Old doesn't mean the same thing that it used
to. The world is full of people who are supposedly old and who are
doing amazing things and having the time of their lives.

Prince Constantin of Lichtenstein became the oldest person to
ride the Cresta run 1998 at the age of eighty-six. Discus thrower
Baba Joginder Singh won the gold medal at the India National
Athletics meeting for Veterans in 1998. He was 105. Yoga teacher
Nena Joyce was happily teaching eight yoga sessions a week at the
Swansea leisure centre and was outraged when she was sacked for
being too old at eighty-two. Leisure World, a community south of

Los Angeles, only admits those over fifty-five and has become the by-word for youthful old age. The 19,000 residents crowd golf courses, swimming pools and tennis courts and attend events put on by over 200 clubs. The average age of residents is seventy-seven and men and women in their nineties work out in the gym and are still enjoying life to the full.

HOW OLD ARE YOU?
Age isn't simply a matter of how many years you have lived. There are three distinct measures of age that you need to take into account when deciding how old you are – and how old you want to be.

- **First**, there's your chronological age: the number of years, months and days you've lived.
- **Second**, there's your biological age, the age your body is, measured in terms of cellular processes and critical life signs.
- **Third**, there's your psychological age, which is simply how old you feel you are.

Only one of these is fixed – your chronological age. And this is the least reliable of the three. One 35-year-old may be as healthy as a man ten years younger, while the next may already have the body of a 50-year-old. Your biological age is a more effective measure, because it shows how time and the life you have lived have affected your organs. But it's also more complex, because some organs may be in great shape while others are not. You might have poor eyesight but great muscle strength, for instance. The older you get the more unique your body becomes, as it evolves into a map of your life.

The age that is really significant is your psychological age. This has a profound influence on your biological age, which can be changed at any time. Adopting a more positive attitude and a healthier lifestyle can reduce your biological age dramatically within weeks.

Your psychological age has no boundaries and can be altered in seconds, simply by the thoughts you choose to entertain. Choose to feel young and adopt a youthful approach and your body will literally grow younger.

EXERCISE

Are you letting yourself be dictated to by your chronological age, and the preconceptions you have about growing old? Take a pen and answer these questions:

1) *How old do I feel?*
2) *How old do I look?*
3) *How often do I talk about growing older, or blame my inability to do something on my age?*
4) *Do I expect to become ill/infirm/put on weight/move less easily as I become older?*
5) *What kind of health do I expect to enjoy at sixty? seventy? eighty?*
6) *Do I believe that old age is a miserable condition?*
7) *Do I believe that life's possibilities grow more restricted as I grow older?*

Well, do you look or feel older than you are? Did you discover a few horribly negative preconceptions that you have about old age? Great. Better to get them all out and have a good look at them. Then we can nail them for good.

THE TRUTH ABOUT AGEING

Your body is constantly renewing itself. Your skin replaces itself once a month, your stomach lining every five days, your liver every six weeks and your entire skeleton every three months. By the end of this year about 98 percent of you will be brand new. And every single one of the millions of cells which make up your body and which constantly replenish themselves, have an inner intelligence.

Ageing is what happens when processes in the body that should remain stable, balanced and self-renewing deviate from their proper course. And this happens simply because we believe that it will and we send this message, unconsciously, to our bodies, which obediently carry out our instructions.

Ageing occurs largely because we expect it to and our bodies get the message, from us, that they are to grow old. We are conditioned from earliest childhood to expect to grow old and to see certain signs of ageing at certain ages. As Deepak Chopra, the world-class pioneer in mind/body medicine says in his book *Ageless Body, Timeless Mind*: 'Ageing seems to be something that's happening to you when in fact it is something your body has largely learned to do.'

Yet wise and youthful people around the world are proving that if you choose consciously to control the messages you give your body you can change what happens to it. There are bodily functions which were, until recently, believed to be out of our conscious control. Things like heart rate, temperature, the operation of internal organs were believed to have their own timing and functioning, independent of us. Yet many stunning examples have now proven that this is not the case. Take Indian holy man Swami Rama. He displayed a remarkable ability to control bodily functions that were thought to be totally automatic, simply by using his awareness. In one instance he caused the skin of one hand to grow warmer while the skin of the other grew colder. After just a couple of minutes one hand was flushed red with warmth and the other was pale grey with cold. The temperature difference between them was ten degrees Farenheit.

Many spiritual traditions teach bodily control to their holy men. Young Tibetan Buddhist monks are expected to demonstrate their bodily control with feats such as sitting on a frozen lake and melting the ice around them with an intense meditational stare. All that is happening in these examples is that the holy men have learned to use their conscious awareness to control what is happening in their bodies. Its something every one of us has the capacity to do.

THE SECRET OF YOUTH

If you want to stay young, to retain a sense of wellbeing and to live a long and healthy life, then you must change the messages you are giving your body – in other words your psychological age. These messages are based on beliefs you accumulated throughout your life. And you are constantly passing them on to your body at a conscious and unconscious level.

Every time you say: 'I'm getting older'; 'My memory's going'; 'I don't have as much energy as I used to'; or 'That's too young for me', your body takes these statements as clear instructions and carries them out. The thoughts, judgements and feelings that move constantly through your mind are the results of your deeply held beliefs. Your fear of ageing and your belief that you must age becomes a self-fulfilling prophecy.

When you change the messages you are giving your body it will respond accordingly. The minute you begin to see yourself as young rather than old, changes will begin to happen in your body. Professor Ellen Langer proved this in a wonderful experiment she carried out in 1979. She and her colleagues at Harvard took a group of old men, all over seventy-five, for a week's retreat at a country resort. When they arrived, the resort had been set up to duplicate life as it had been twenty years earlier. There were magazines, photographs and music from that era. The men were asked to behave as if it were 1959, discussing their jobs, families and politics as they were twenty years younger. A control group was sent on a similar retreat, but without the time reversal. During the week Langer and her team made extensive measurements of the subjects' ages. They wanted to discover whether seeing oneself as old or young directly influences the ageing process.

The results were remarkable. Compared with the control group, the 1959 group showed a number of signs of age reversal. Their memories and manual dexterity improved. They became more active and self-sufficient and their faces looked visibly younger by an average of three years. Even aspects of ageing that were considered irreversible changed. Finger length tends to shorten with age, but these men's fingers had lengthened; stiffened joints became more flexible and their postures straightened. Their muscle strength, hearing and vision improved, too. Over half the group improved their IQ scores.

This landmark study proved beyond doubt that behaving as though you are younger and being treated as though you are younger will actually *make* you younger.

Exercise

I want you rigorously to examine the way you talk to yourself and others about ageing. What phrases do you use? What judgements do you project? What restrictions do you accept?

How often do you tell yourself that something is too young for you, that you're past it, that you'll look like 'mutton dressed as lamb', that you've got to accept being more tired, feeling stiffer, being forgetful, going grey?

How often do you stop yourself from doing something because of your age? Do you use it as an excuse for avoiding a job opportunity, a date or an adventure? How often do you wish you'd done something when you were younger? How often do you get up in the morning and look in the mirror and tell yourself you're getting older and looking worse?

I want you to root out all this ageist behaviour and toss it out of the window right now. I insist that you banish all ageing statements, all possible references to you or anyone else growing old and all excuses based on age.

From now on I want you to look and feel the age you *want* to be. I long ago stopped telling people my age. When people ask me how old I am I ask them how old they think I am. Inevitably they name an age younger than my chronological age and I simply smile and agree with them. Society is so determined to label everyone with an age and all the judgements that go with that age.

'Fancy doing that at her/his age?' we hear.

I want you to stop going along with this pigeon-holing, destructive behaviour and to free yourself and others from age restrictions. Stop thinking decay and decline. Be the age you want to be and live, think, act and dress accordingly.

GILLIAN'S STORY

GILLIAN CAME TO ME BECAUSE SHE FELT HER LIFE WAS STUCK IN A RUT. SHE WAS BEING PASSED OVER FOR PROMOTION AT WORK AND HADN'T BEEN ON A DATE IN TWO YEARS. SHE WAS FORTY-ONE BUT SHE DESCRIBED THE LIFESTYLE OF A PERSON MUCH, MUCH OLDER. SHE DRESSED IN CLOTHES WHICH WERE, FRANKLY, FRUMPY. EVEN THOUGH SHE HAD A GOOD FIGURE, SHE WORE DULL GREYS AND BEIGES AND VERY UNADVENTUROUS STYLES. HER HAIR AND MAKE-UP WERE THE SAME — AN UNFLATTERING CUT AND NO LIPSTICK OR BRIGHT COLOURS.

THE MORE WE TALKED, THE MORE I REALISED THAT GILLIAN SAW HERSELF AS BEING OLD. SHE FREQUENTLY REFERRED TO HER AGE AND

SAW IT AS A BARRIER TO THE JOB AND THE RELATIONSHIP SHE WANTED. SHE FELT SHE WAS ALREADY ON A DOWNHILL SLOPE INTO OLD AGE AND INFIRMITY. I ASKED GILLIAN WHETHER SHE WAS PREPARED TO MAKE SOME DRAMATIC CHANGES AND SHE AGREED TO FOLLOW MY INSTRUCTIONS TO THE LETTER, NO MATTER HOW RELUCTANT SHE FELT. I BEGAN BY ASKING HER TO ELIMINATE ALL AGEING REFERENCES FROM HER INNER AND OUTER DIALOGUE AND TO REPLACE THEM WITH YOUTHFUL REFERENCES. SHE WAS TO THINK OF HERSELF AND REFER TO HERSELF AS YOUNG AND ENERGETIC.

NEXT WE WENT TO WORK ON HER WARDROBE, HAIR AND MAKE-UP. SHE SPLASHED OUT ON A GORGEOUS, SMART HAIRCUT AND WENT TO A COLOUR CONSULTANT TO FIND OUT WHAT COLOURS MADE HER LOOK FANTASTIC. IT TURNED OUT THAT GILLIAN'S 'WOW' COLOURS WERE BRIGHT RED, PURPLE AND BLUE AND AS SOON AS SHE TOSSED OUT THE OLD, DRAB CLOTHES AND BEGAN TO WEAR HER NEW COLOURS, THEY TOOK TEN YEARS OFF HER AGE. NEXT I ASKED GILLIAN TO START MIXING WITH SOME YOUNGER PEOPLE AND GOING TO SOME FUN, HIP PLACES. MUCH TO HER SURPRISE GILLIAN HAD A GREAT TIME AND LOVED HER NEW LOOK AND STYLE. WITHIN A MONTH SHE WAS TRANSFORMED AND FRIENDS WERE ASKING HER WHAT WAS HER SECRET FOR LOOKING YEARS YOUNGER. THE PROMOTION SHE WANTED AND A NEW BOYFRIEND BOTH ARRIVED SOON AFTERWARDS.

SIXTY IS THE NEW FORTY

I want you to think, act and talk young, just as Gillian did. Go through your wardrobe with a critical eye and throw out anything that makes you look old. Times have changed. Sixty is the new forty; fifty is the new thirty. Lulu is a great example of this: at fifty going on thirty-four. Her figure is great, her hair gorgeous and she exudes energy and a love of life. She wears chic little leather jackets and trousers, does demanding dance routines with men thirty years younger and looks wonderful. Compare her to some of the other fifty-year-olds on TV, a few of whom look as though they've raided their granny's wardrobe for safe little outfits to wear.

Susan Sarandon is another glowing example of youthful looks. At fifty-three she looks thirty-five. She has refused plastic surgery, unlike so many other actresses her age, and she has a hugely successful career – all her best films have been made since she was forty – and a relationship with actor Tim Robbins who is twelve years her junior. Susan summed up her attitude to ageing when she said: 'I'd rather work on the inside, on lifting my spirits instead of my face.'

Absolutely. Feeling joyful and optimistic knocks years off in an instant. Think of those times you've fallen madly in love and how it makes you glow and sparkle with vitality. That's what I want for you, from now on.

Here are some of the affirming statements I want you to become familiar with and to use often:

- *I am full of energy.*
- *I enjoy vibrant good health.*
- *I feel young, strong and alive.*
- *I have a great memory.*
- *I look much younger than my actual age.*
- *I can look good in any clothes I enjoy wearing.*
- *I feel younger every day.*
- *I look better and better every day.*

Add some of your own and use them every time you feel tempted to resort to one of those miserable ageing statements.

STOP THE CLOCK

It's entirely possible to slow down the ageing process. It's also possible, as Ellen Langer's experiment (see page 194) proved, to turn the clock back and *reverse* some of the signs of ageing. Take a good look at yourself and decide exactly what you'd like to change and what you'd like to keep. What ageing signs would you like to slow down or reverse? Think it can't be done? Just suspend your disbelief, follow my ten-point 'Stop the Clock' plan for looking fabulously young, and prepare to be stunned and thrilled.

ACT YOUNG

If you want to appear young then you must behave as though you are young. Look at a small child and you'll notice that they never keep still. They're moving around all the time, full of boundless energy. Learn from them and refuse to slow down. Nothing is more ageing than feeling that you're physically unable to move. The old people who wither away fast are the ones who sit in chairs and refuse to move for the rest of their lives. So keep moving. Bound up and down stairs, dance, walk, run, feel the pleasure of having a body and being able to use it. Remind yourself that there is absolutely no need to slow down as you grow older. There are plenty of ninety-year-old marathon runners around to prove the point.

Dress in clothes that make you feel young, too. There are no age restrictions on clothes anymore. If you feel good in something, wear it. If it looks good, that's good enough. Ignore any sour-grapes reactions. Go to fun funky shops and avoid the boring, safe middle-of-the-road ones.

Take interior designer and socialite Nicky Haslam, sixty-one, as an example. Three years ago he ditched his grey pompadour hairstyle for a short black crop, had a face-lift, started dressing like a wayward teenager and transformed his life. He didn't give a damn what anyone thought of his new look, saying: 'Well I don't want to dress like my mother, I just try to be contemporary.'

KEEP YOUNG COMPANY

We take on the behaviour of those we spend most time with. If we hang out with much older people we'll begin to feel and behave older. A woman I know proved this point to me vividly. She had been married to a friend of mine and had been a young, fun and hip person who dressed in great clothes and loved to throw parties.

I met her again recently and could hardly believe the change. She left my friend for a man fifteen years older than her and after four years with him she had aged dramatically. Gone were the fun clothes and the great hairstyle. She wore dull colours and had grown her hair into an unflattering, ageing style. She had put on weight and lost her sparkle. She'd given up throwing parties – he didn't like them – and had taken up gardening and knitting. Nothing wrong with gardening or knitting, unless they've become a substitute for having a life.

Make sure that you spend plenty of time with younger people. Hang out with a group of friends who have fun together, go to great places that make you feel good.

CHANGE YOUR VIEWS ABOUT BEING OLD

How do you see old people? Do you imagine that most of them are just sitting around in nursing homes waiting to die? That their life is effectively over? That once you hit sixty there's no point in trying anything new? Well, think again. The truth is that there are no more old people than young ones in nursing homes or long-term care. Only five percent of old people need institutionalised care, just as only five percent of young people do.

More and more old people are still at home, still enjoying life and still doing new and interesting things. To write them off or patronise them is a huge mistake. And who's old anyway? Elizabeth Taylor, flouncing round the world on the arm of Michael Jackson in baby-doll tops trimmed with feathers? At sixty-nine she's well past pension age but she can still bring a room full of people to a standstill just by walking into it. Joan Collins, another pensioner of sixty-eight, is still dating a man fifteen years younger and looking stunningly sexy and glamorous. There is absolutely no reason why everyone can't age in the same way. These superstars don't give a damn about the age in their passports; they're out there living life and making sure they look damn good while they do it. And more and more older people are doing the same.

GO WITH THE FLOW

The personality type that ages fastest is the A-type – the driven perfectionists who think they have to do everything themselves and who can't bear to give up control of anything. If this is you then it's time to loosen up and understand that there's more to life than struggle. This type of person suffers from a lot of stress and is often irritable and difficult to be around. They are not necessarily the highest achievers and certainly aren't the happiest people.

So let go of trying to be perfect or having all the answers and live a little more. The danger with type A is that life passes you by while you're trying to get everything on your list done.

What do I mean by live? Have fun, try an adventure, do something you've always wanted to do, laugh, feel the wind in your hair, anything, in fact, that makes you notice the world around you and enjoy it.

Teach yourself to take life lightly. Don't make every event into a crisis. Save your adrenaline for a *real* emergency and try shrugging your shoulders and moving on when things go wrong. Psychologist Geoff Lowe and immunologist John Greenman of Hull University carried out a study that they presented to the British Psychological Society in Spring 2000. By testing a number of volunteers they were able to discover that guilty feelings actually lower the immune system. Dr Lowe's conclusion was simple: 'We should be more positive about taking pleasure, especially in everyday simple things.'

Be more adaptable and open to change. Studies of those who live to ninety or one hundred have shown that they cope easily with stress, change and disappointment, bouncing back quickly when things go wrong. So decide right now to build high levels of adaptability into your personality and to be creative about the way you deal with challenging situations.

EXERCISE

The effect of regular exercise on the ageing process is mind-blowing. Regular physical exercise can reverse ten of the most typical effects of ageing, including high blood pressure, excess body fat, improper sugar balance and decreased muscle mass. And the good news is that it's never too late to start. Studies of the elderly have shown that beginning exercise programmes, alongside healthy eating, can improve their life expectancy by ten years.

A team from Tufts University in the US took a group of frail old people, aged between eighty-seven and ninety-six, from a nursing home and put them on a weight-training programme. To every-one's astonishment, far from keeling over exhausted, they thrived on it and within eight weeks wasted muscle had come back by 300 percent. Their co-ordination and balance had also improved and they were all enjoying a more active life. Some of them had been unable to walk unaided before the programme began. After it, they could get to the bathroom alone, an act of independence that also restored their dignity.

What's more, exercise is great for your sex life. Researchers at the Newcastle University Medical School found that older men who take regular exercise have far higher levels of the male sex hormone testosterone, which is the biggest single determinant of sex drive in men. Levels of this hormone decrease with age, resulting in the loss of sex drive and potency. But in men aged fifty-five to sixty-five who ran more than forty miles a week they discovered that the testosterone levels were still high. If this isn't enough to convince you to get down to your nearest gym this minute, then remember that exercise also releases endorphins, the chemicals in the brain which help you feel good.

Choose exercise that you can enjoy, whether it's swimming, running, squash, working out or taking classes. I recommend that you take up yoga as well. Those who do yoga regularly often look years younger – look at Raquel Welch, who at fifty swears by it and looks at least fifteen years younger. Apart from being great for your mind and your body, yoga makes you feel younger because you end up with a fantastically supple body and able to do things no one else can do, like stand on your head.

Learning to exercise regularly is just like learning any other new habit. The only secret is to do it and keep doing it until not doing it feels odd. This can take anywhere between two weeks and three months. So commit today to a three-month exercise programme and stick to it, whether you feel like doing it or not. Forget about being in the mood, having the time or the energy. Just do it.

DRINK MORE WATER
One of the greatest single causes of ageing is dehydration. The world is full of people who feel tired, ill, old and unhappy simply

because they aren't drinking enough water. Shocking but true. Chronic dehydration is considered, in some parts of the world, to be one of the leading causes of death in old age. Too little water can lead to a whole host of conditions, including kidney failure, heart attacks, blackouts, dizziness, lethargy and even senile dementia.

There are plenty of people around looking for complex reasons for overwhelming feelings of malaise and fatigue. They convince themselves that they must have some awful medical condition when all they actually need is water. Don't be one of them. Eight glasses of water a day will give your body an enormous health boost. Your skin will look clear, your eyes bright and your energy will improve.

Psychotherapist Christine Webber says in her book *Get the Happiness Habit*: 'Frequently, when we feel irritable and grotty, we're actually dehydrated. And quite often when we reach for food – in the belief that we're hungry – we're really thirsty instead.'

Try the 'pale pee' test. If you're drinking enough water your urine should be almost colourless. No other drink is a substitute for water; your body will have to extract water from other drinks and tea and coffee will actually dehydrate you further. Drink water, and lots of it.

MEDITATE

OK, we all know meditation is good for the spirit and will help you to feel clearer and calmer. But here's the truly amazing bonus. Regular meditation will knock years off your age. It has now been established, scientifically, that long-term meditators can knock between five and twelve years off their chronological age. Why? Because when you meditate your body begins to function more efficiently. Your breathing, oxygen consumption and metabolism all slow down. And the result is that the hormonal imbalance associated with stress – which is known to speed up the ageing process – is reversed. Meditation has always been a way of life in the East, but it's now becoming hugely popular in the West and there are books, tapes and classes everywhere.

So, if you think you don't have time to meditate or meditation seems too hard, make the time and do it anyway. Like getting enough exercise and drinking water, it's simply a question of adopting a new habit.

THINK ABOUT OTHERS

One of the great antidotes to old age and ill-health is to be more giving. A study carried out by Larry Scherwitz of the University of California beautifully illustrates this. He tapes the conversations of 600 old men, counting the number of times each said 'I', 'me' or 'mine'. A third of the old men were suffering from heart disease. When the results of the tapes were compared with the frequency of heart disease he found that the men who said 'I', 'me' or 'mine' most often had the highest risk of heart trouble.

Scherwitz followed the men's progress for several years and discovered that the more a man habitually talked about himself, the more likely he was to have a coronary. His conclusion was that the less you open your heart to others, the more your heart suffers.

British Lottery winner Ray Wragg is a great example of how being generous makes you happier. Unlike many other lottery winners who have complained that it made them miserable coming into a fortune, Ray enjoyed his fortune immensely, because he gave most of it away. Ray, a 62-year-old supervisor for a construction company, won £7.6 million in January 2000. Over the next few months he and his wife Barbara gave away £5 million – two-thirds – of his win and helped to make the dreams of those closest to them come true. Not only did they make sure that their own three children and their five grandchildren were secure for life, they helped ten friends to retire early and gave large sums to three hospitals in their home town of Sheffield in the UK.

Ray said: 'Obviously a win like this is bound to have an effect on your lives, but we decided straightaway that it would change the lives of lots of other people around us. I could have bought a yacht or a racehorse, but I couldn't see the point. We've got a new house and a Range Rover and that is enough for us. Thanks to our win we've been able to make life much more comfortable and enjoyable for the people who are dearest to us and to help people in Sheffield. I've read about some lottery millionaires who have been made miserable by all their money, but it has made us happy because it has made a lot of other people very happy.'

Loneliness is another major factor in old age. Studies have shown that those who live alone for several years or more tend to age faster. So connect with other people, have relationships, be generous, go out of your way to do something for others, and help out where you can. I'm not suggesting that you become a dogsbody or spend your life hanging around busy roads hoping to help old ladies across. Just take your mind off yourself on a regular basis by thinking about others, and cultivate generosity in yourself.

HAVE GOALS AND A PURPOSE
Having something to live for makes you more likely to live longer. And so does a sense of achievement as you reach the goals you have set yourself. Never stop setting yourself new goals and challenges, and working steadily towards them. Choose targets that stretch you but are still attainable. Make sure they excite and inspire you.

Don't put things off or tell yourself *I'll get round to it one day*. Let that day be today. Don't become an old person who lives with bitter regret. I said at the start of this book that I realised very young how terrible it must be to live with regret. I am so grateful for that realisation, because it's spurred me on through at least three careers so far! I wouldn't dream of putting things off or planning them for a few years' time. I'm not interested in excuses; I begin doing the things I want to do right now and I'm always discovering new things I want to try or new heights I want to reach. To live without regret is to choose a life of action, of decision, of adventure. Join me.

TAKE RESPONSIBILITY FOR YOUR HEALTH

If you want to stay young then you need to stay healthy. Looking young means looking well, with clear, sparkling eyes and skin and a fit body at the right weight.

Taking responsibility for your own health means two things. Firstly, that you must do everything in your power to get yourself healthy. And, secondly, that you must take responsibility for bringing yourself back to health if you are ill.

Be Healthy. Keeping yourself healthy means eating well, getting enough sleep and exercise and refusing to use drugs or take excess alcohol. There is a Chinese saying: 'The time to start digging a well is before you feel thirsty. And the time to start attending to your health is before you fall sick.'

To eat well you must give your body what it needs, not what you have trained your tastebuds to like. This doesn't mean eating things you hate, but it does mean re-training yourself, if necessary, to like things which benefit you. If you are overweight then it's important to lose the excess, not with ridiculous or crippling diets, but by eating healthy, balanced meals so that your body will regain it's natural rhythm and balance.

The myth that you can be fat and happy is just that – a myth. I've never met a person yet who feels great buried inside rolls of fat or looking like a whale. Overweight people usually feel pretty bad about themselves and put their health at risk. Plenty of therapists and fat people, especially women, have told us that fat is beautiful and that fat people ought to love themselves. But a recent survey by *Slimming Magazine* only confirmed what most of us already knew – that many fat women feel miserable about it. I don't doubt that many fat men do, too.

What's more, several famous fat women who insisted they loved being that way have now lost the weight and admit that they've never felt happier. UK TV presenter Vanessa Feltz lost five stone (31 kg) after her husband left her, and she proudly posed in swimsuits to show off her new size twelve figure. She also looked ten years younger. In the US, Roseanne Barr shed several stone and also told us she felt a whole lot better. John Travolta looked miserable and bloated and his career nose-dived when he piled on the pounds. He lost the weight, looked years younger and his career soared again.

If you're fat and pretending to be OK about it, then give up the pretence and lose the weight instead. There's no greater feeling than having a body of which you *really* feel proud. You'll also lose years along with the stones because fat is ageing.

I want you to forget about food and binge on life. If you're fat and unhappy it's because you're suppressing your vitality. You're stuck, fearful and avoiding risks. When fat people come to me I ask them: 'What's eating you?' and it's never to do with food. I was recently asked to help an overweight woman on the UK morning TV programme GMTV. She had put on three stone (19kg) since retiring. I told her to get busy and get a life, not a diet. She agreed that I was right; she'd stopped cycling around and started over-eating because she had nothing to do. When I suggested she get a job she told me she was too old. Not true! I pointed out that plenty of people her age were working, so she put an ad in the local paper, offering herself as a Mrs Doubtfire for a family. Of course she was inundated with offers. Within weeks of starting her job the weight fell off without her even noticing.

Every single study on rejuvenation comes to the conclusion that the youthful old eat less. Some naturopaths suggest that you should eat no more than two handfuls of food per meal. This is as much as you need and will free vast amounts of energy for other things. *Never* eat until you feel full, sluggish or bloated. Eat small meals more often and make sure that what you eat is of the highest possible quality and nutritional value. If you want to feel alive and full of energy, and to start each day with a buzz, then feed yourself nutritious, organic, whole foods and loads of fruit and vegetables.

Eating a healthy diet, which means lots of fruit and veg, wholegrains and low-fat meat and dairy produce, has also been scientifically proven to reduce by 30 percent your chances of having heart disease or cancer. Christine Webber suggests that if you eat a lot of junk food and don't know where to start then begin by eating five pieces of fruit a day, no matter what else you eat. You'll notice the good effects of the extra vitamins and roughage, and this will encourage you to make other improvements.

Getting enough sleep is important, too. Prolonged lack of sleep leaves you unhealthy, irritable and miserable. You'll look grey and have no energy. Most people need eight hours a night and get less. If you feel continually tired, start with some extra sleep and see if it makes a difference. It almost certainly will because a lot of so-called fatigue syndromes are simply lack of sleep.

Drugs, of any kind, are off the menu if you want to stay healthy and young. Prolonged prescription drugs such as tranquillisers and anti-depressants are just as bad as some recreational drugs.

Whatever you're on, come off it as soon as you possibly can unless it's vital for a medical condition. If you're drug-free then great. Stay that way.

Alcohol can be fun, but know your limits. Closet drunks are a bore and they look dire. If you get drunk more than once in a blue moon then set yourself a two-drink limit and stick to it. Swap to soft drinks and see it as an investment in your future.

Never, ever simply turn yourself over to someone else to be cured. To put all your faith in the hands of doctors is to give up being a responsible adult. Take responsibility by getting involved in your own diagnosis and recovery and by keeping yourself healthy in the first place. Doctors often do great things, but they're not always right or careful and there are other types of practitioners who can be far more effective in many cases.

Remember that doctors are concerned with sickness, not health and get yourself a health practitioner instead.

In ancient China doctors were paid to keep people well. Sadly that's not the case now, so it's important to find a practitioner who will support you in increasing your level of wellness.

If you're ill, ask yourself why. Illness is always the body's way of giving us a message. What's yours telling you? Trust your own instinct. No one knows more about you, your life and health than you do. It may be that what you need is rest, a change of scene, a decision or a fresh start. If a job, a house or a relationship is making you ill, move away from it.

Use the vast array of complementary health practitioners to support you in making and keeping yourself well. Try homoeopathy, reflexology, Tibetan healing, shiatsu massage, cranial osteopathy, acupuncture, naturopathy, herbalism or kinesieology. Try one at a time, to see which one works best for you. Make it your business to find out about complementary healing. Talk to other people about it, find out what works for them and get recommendations.

Never forget your body's remarkable ability to heal itself. Trust yourself to know what you need, find people you like and trust to help you heal and never accept that any condition is beyond help.

YOUR ASSIGNMENT

I want you to decide, right now, what age you were when you were at your most excited and energetic. This is the age I want you to aim for and live into. I want to you talk, dress, think and be that age. If you do it really well then people will soon begin to think you are that age.

Ask other people regularly how old they think you are. The closer they get to your perfect age, the better you're doing. If they're still a couple of years off, then you know you've still got a bit of work to do.

Go do it!

AND REMEMBER . . .

The age you feel is the one which counts.
  You can change that age at any moment.
  Your body will stay young if you give it youthful messages.
  Looking young means looking well.
  To look well you must keep yourself healthy.
  If you're healthy you'll have boundless energy.
  With boundless energy you can create anything you want.

CHAPTER TEN

WHEN THE GOING GETS TOUGH, THE TOUGH GET TOUGHER

NOW THAT you're out there taking giant steps to live the life you really want, you need to get comfortable with failure! Why? Because failure is a requirement for success. Ask any hugely successful person how many times they've failed on the way to their goals and they'll tell you 'plenty'. How often have you heard of famous authors, singers, politicians and entrepreneurs who were turned down or turned away dozens of times before doors began to open for them. What marks these people out is that they weren't afraid of failure. They dusted themselves off and carried on every time until they succeeded. So if you want to be really successful you need to learn to take failure in your stride.

What makes most people fail is not failure itself but the fear of failure. Failure itself makes you stronger, but the fear of failure paralyses you and stops you from even trying in the first place. It holds you back more than any other single thing and is the commonest 'bogeyman' I've encountered in people from all divides.

What people who fear failure don't realise is that it is indispensable for success. You simply cannot succeed without failing. In fact, the very process of failing and learning from that failure brings you closer to success. Look at the amazing examples of successful people who simply refused to accept failure. Colonel Sanders was sixty-five and on his state pension when he decided to do something with his only asset – a great chicken recipe. He went from one food outlet to another and was turned down by an astonishing 1009 people before he found someone who agreed to take his recipe. It became Kentucky Fried Chicken (KFC).

Walt Disney who was turned down by 300 banks before he finally persuaded one to give him the funding for Disneyworld. He didn't give up after the first hundred nos, or even the second hundred and that's how he became such a success.

That's why, at this stage on our journey together, I want you to learn to handle the notions and the fear of failure so that they don't haunt you and hold you back in the way they do countless others. Forewarned is always forearmed. What I want to do in this chapter is to alert you to your own fear of failure, your personal comfort zone, and then to equip you with the tools and the know-how to take you beyond both. I will show you, with the help of some inspiring people's stories, that there is no such thing as failure – only the meaning that we choose to give to events; in other words, the lessons we learn from them and the choices we make with what we have learned.

Let me tell you about a man whose courage in the face of failure was amazing.

GEORGE'S STORY

A FEW YEARS AGO GEORGE STRATFORD WAS SLEEPING ON THE STREETS. NOW, AT THE AGE OF FIFTY-FIVE, HE IS AN AWARD-

WINNING AD MAN AT THE WORLD'S MOST FAMOUS AD AGENCY,
SAATCHI AND SAATCHI.

SIX YEARS EARLIER GEORGE WAS AT HIS LOWEST EBB. HE HAD
BEEN UNEMPLOYED FOR MORE THAN THREE YEARS AND COULDN'T
EVEN FIND WORK AS A TOILET CLEANER. ALMOST FIFTY AND WITH
NO FORMAL QUALIFICATIONS HE HAD LOST HIS WELL-PAID JOB AS A
FRENCH POLISHER AND WAS SCRAPING BY ON BENEFITS. HE WAS
ALONE AFTER THE DEATH OF HIS MOTHER, HIS SAVINGS WERE GONE
AND SO WAS HIS HOPE. 'I NEVER CONTEMPLATED SUICIDE,' HE
RECALLS. 'BUT THERE WERE TIMES WHEN I COULDN'T GIVE A SHIT IF
I HAD A HEART ATTACK AND DROPPED DEAD, BECAUSE THERE WAS
NOTHING LEFT IN LIFE FOR ME.'

YET TODAY GEORGE'S LIFE HAS CHANGED BEYOND RECOGNITION.
NOT ONLY IS HE MAKING HIS MARK IN AN EXCITING NEW CAREER,
HE HAS GOT MARRIED AND PUBLISHED HIS FIRST NOVEL, TOO.
GEORGE'S EXTRAORDINARY TALE STARTED WHEN HE'D LOST HIS JOB
AND NO ONE ELSE WOULD TAKE HIM ON BECAUSE HE WAS TOO OLD
AND HAD NO QUALIFICATIONS. HE WAS TOTALLY BROKE AND HIS
GLOOM DEEPENED. 'I WOKE UP ONE MORNING AND THOUGHT:
"WHAT WOULD MUM THINK IF SHE COULD SEE THIS BUM I'VE
TURNED INTO?"' HE SAYS. HE DECIDED TO DO SOMETHING ABOUT
IT. SO HE TOOK AND PASSED AN ENGLISH A LEVEL AND THEN
APPLIED FOR AN ADVERTISING AND COPYWRITING COURSE.

AT FIRST THE COLLEGE AUTHORITIES SAID HE WAS WASTING HIS
TIME BECAUSE OF HIS AGE, BUT THEY CHANGED THEIR MINDS WHEN
THEY SAW HIS WRITTEN WORK. EVEN SO, HIS TUTOR TOLD HIM
THAT NO MATTER HOW WELL HE DID ON THE COURSE, NO ONE
WOULD EMPLOY HIM BECAUSE HE WAS TOO OLD. UNDETERRED,
GEORGE PUSHED FOR A PLACEMENT WITH SAATCHI AND SAATCHI
AND, WHEN HE GOT IT, HE WENT TO EXTRAORDINARY LENGTHS TO
TAKE IT UP.

THE TRAIN FARE TO LONDON TOOK THE LAST OF HIS MONEY AND GEORGE WAS FORCED TO SLEEP ROUGH ON THE STREETS FOR THE THREE NIGHTS HE WAS THERE BECAUSE HE COULDN'T AFFORD A PLACE TO STAY.

'I HID MY SUITCASE UNDER THE DESK AND WHEN EVERYONE LEFT IN THE EVENING I'D HANG AROUND AS LATE AS POSSIBLE UNDER THE PRETENCE OF WORKING. I WOULD COME INTO THE OFFICE AROUND 6 AM AND HAVE A WASH AND BY THE TIME EVERYONE ELSE CAME IN I WAS READY FOR WORK.

'I'D DECIDED THEY MAY NOT EMPLOY ME BUT THERE WAS NO WAY THEY WERE GOING TO FORGET ME. I WROTE NINETEEN RADIO ADS FOR ONE PRODUCER IN TWO DAYS. NONE OF THEM WERE USED, BUT IT SHOWED ENTHUSIASM.'

ANOTHER COMMERCIAL GEORGE WROTE, FOR A BEER, WAS USED AND LATER WON AN AWARD. THE AGENCY OFFERED HIM A THREE-MONTH TRIAL AND THEN A FULL-TIME JOB. SOON AFTERWARDS HE MET 'GIFTY', A RADIO PRODUCER WHO IS NOW HIS WIFE.

GEORGE'S CRISIS CAME WHEN HE LOST A JOB, BUT HE TURNED HIS MISFORTUNE INTO AN OPPORTUNITY TO TRANSFORM HIS LIFE. HE NEVER GAVE UP ON HIMSELF AND HE REFUSED TO LISTEN TO ALL THE EXPERTS AROUND HIM WHO TOLD HIM IT WAS TOO LATE OR THAT HE WAS TOO OLD AND UNEMPLOYABLE. ABOVE ALL, GEORGE WAS PERSISTENT AND FOUND INGENIOUS WAYS TO GET ROUND ALL THE OBSTACLES IN HIS PATH. HE REFUSED TO BE CRUSHED BY HAVING TO SLEEP ROUGH AND MADE SURE HE NEVER LOOKED AS THOUGH HE'D JUST SPENT THE NIGHT ON A PARK BENCH. GEORGE WAS UNSTOPPABLE. HE FELT THAT HE HAD ONE FINAL CHANCE IN LIFE AND NOTHING AND NO ONE WAS GOING TO STOP HIM. HE WAS LIKE A GUIDED MISSILE, ALTERING HIS COURSE AS NEEDED BUT KEEPING HIS TARGET RESOLUTELY IN HIS SIGHTS. HIS LIFE DEPENDED ON THE SUCCESS OF HIS MISSION.

LIFE IS TOO SHORT TO BE AFRAID

Your life and your happiness depend on whether you can muster the same depths of persistence, fearlessness, adaptability and resourcefulness as George. You must live as though your life depends on it. You may not be in the kind of extreme situation George was in but you still need to live your life with a feeling of urgency. You need to make your happiness matter so much that you are pushed to confront your fears and your fear of failure and to take the risks anyway.

TAKE MORE RISKS!

I want you to cultivate the mindset of a natural risk-taker; to keep on reaching, keep on doing until you get what you want and dream about. I want you to be the sort of person who won't settle for 'a bird in the hand' if it's not the right bird. Let others be the ones who settle for what they don't want at the first hurdle, as soon as the going gets a little difficult. Most people prefer to stay within their own personal comfort zones where they avoid uncertainty and discomfort, even if this means that they never reach for their dreams. Your comfort zone is the area of life in which you feel at home and familiar. It's safe, predictable and easily manageable. Many people step quickly back into their comfort zones the minute they've put a toe outside it because they just can't tolerate the discomfort. They'll turn down the possibilities and opportunities that stepping outside their comfort zone would bring.

Comfort and familiarity are the enemies of momentum. They seduce you into a false sense of ease and keep you in a place where you avoid the stress, pressure and fear of risking and possibly failing. But for those who are willing to step beyond their comfort zones the rewards are magnificent. In 1990, at the age of fifty-eight, the actor Brian Blessed climbed Everest alone and became the oldest man to reach the height of 28,000 feet. He fulfilled the dream he'd had since he was fourteen. Since then he has made two more assaults on Everest as well as climbing Mount Kilimanjaro, Aconcagua in the Andes and, most recently, Mount Roraima in Venezuela.

'We all have our own Everests to climb,' he says. 'You've just got to go for it. If I hadn't at least tried, I would always have been unfulfilled. I think the greatest danger in life is not taking chances. There are so many knockers, so many negative people wanting to grind you down, but you can't let them. If people say you are mad, you know you're on the right track.'

WHY LEAVE YOUR COMFORT ZONE?

You may well ask why you should bother to leave your comfort zone if it's so warm and cosy there. I'll give you three good reasons.

The first is that you will *have* to leave it sometime, however hard you resist. No one has an entirely safe life with no upheaval or shocks. Uncertainty is a fact of life, the one thing you can rely on. A quiet, uneventful life without turbulence is just not an option, however much you might wish for it. Something, somewhere, some time is going to test you beyond what you already know and beyond what you're comfortable with. Life is not about wrapping yourself in cotton wool and getting by as quietly as possible. That's not living, it's just tip-toeing around life. There is no escaping life outside the comfort zone. It will happen, if it hasn't already. Far better, then, that you have already chosen to step outside, rather than being hurled out when you least expect it. When crises do happen, you'll have the experience and understanding to deal with them.

The second reason is this: I believe that as human beings we instinctively look for ways of refining ourselves and of honing, fine-tuning and upgrading who we are. We have an inbuilt capacity and a powerful drive to improve on the original prototype of who we are. And it is only through stretching and testing ourselves that we have the scope to do this. It's no coincidence that personal development courses increasingly include outward bound challenges as part of their programmes, provoking people to go way beyond their 'safe' limits, through abseiling down cliff faces, canoeing through rapids or bungee jumping off bridges. I recently took part in one of these courses and walked on hot coals as my fear-busting challenge! And I can tell you that there is no greater feeling of euphoria and personal power than sashaying barefoot down that runway of glowing coals.

Many of the people there that night totally transformed their comfort zones in the seconds it took to take that walk. They woke the next morning better versions of themselves, revved-up, turbo-charged models of the previous day's standard archetype. Life will never be the same for them as they confront the fears in all other areas of their lives. After all, when you've walked on fire and survived, what else could overwhelm you?

People talk of the Second World War with such nostalgia. It was a time when ordinary people displayed extraordinary bravery, courage and spirit. The term 'Dunkirk spirit' has become part of the English language, celebrating forever the time when thousands of people sailed from Britain in every available boat, no matter how tiny, across the channel to rescue the troops from the French beaches. Over a seven-day period in late May and early June 1940, 338,226 troops, trapped on the beaches by the German forces, were evacuated from Dunkirk by 222 naval ships and 665 civilian craft. In particular, the role of the 'little ships' has passed into legend. There were tugboats and fishing boats, coasters and trawlers, lifeboats and paddle boats, river cruisers and paddle steamers. Between them this improvised fleet rescued more than 80,000 men from certain capture or death.

Older people sometimes say that young people today wouldn't do the same thing, that their calibre is poorer. Not true. People were superhuman during the war because they *had* to be. Circumstances brought out their brilliance and bravery and took them way beyond their comfort zones. The quickest way to find those hidden depths of brilliance tucked away inside you and to activate your nobility, your genius and your bottomless courage is to create some massive, meaningful tasks for yourself. Live a safe, predictable life and you'll never know just how extraordinary you really are. Make the circumstances of your life challenging enough to draw your greatness to the surface.

As philosopher Michel de Montaigne said over 400 years ago: 'To compose our character is our duty . . . Our great and glorious masterpiece is to live appropriately. All other things, to rule, to lay up treasure, to build, are at most but little appendices and props.'

Look at British nurse Sally Becker who became known as the Angel of Mostar by driving lorries of food and supplies through war-torn Bosnia and rescuing many children. Or Erin Brockovich, whose story was made into a film after she won a multi-million pound settlement for a community in the United States after exposing a major health hazard cover-up.

Are Sally Becker or Erin Brockovich fundamentally any different from you? Absolutely not, but they stand out from the crowd because they did extraordinary things. You can, too, any time you choose. Don't wait for a war or a crisis. Create your own urgency. Create the right conditions for your own brilliance to emerge. As President John Kennedy said:

Without belittling the courage with which men have died, we should not forget those acts of courage with which men have lived. The courage of life is often a less dramatic spectacle than the courage of the final moment, but it is no less a magnificent mixture of triumph and tragedy. A man does what he must in spite of personal consequences, in spite of obstacles and dangers and pressures – that is the basis of all human morality . . .

The third reason for leaving your comfort zone is simply that you get to live a far more interesting life if you do. You don't want a dreary, predictable life. I know you don't because you would never have picked up this book if you weren't enticed by the idea of living your ideal life and being the best you can be. You are the sort of person who doesn't want to miss opportunities and accumulate regrets. You have the drive to make your life count, to make it as meaningful as possible. You want to spend yourself well. You know that life is precious, that it doesn't go on forever, that you must make every day count, that it's all down to you to make it work and make whatever you want happen.

Given that this is the sort of person you are, living a cosy life inside that comfort zone is just not an option. You know you can't pretend to yourself, that you can't hide away your longing to live the life of your dreams, desires and grand ambitions. A restricted, suppressed life is not for you.

This is your call to arms. Bring your hidden, unspoken desires off the back burner and right to the table. Give them centre stage and rekindle vast amounts of passion for them. Forget about avoiding risks. A grand life, a big life with a juicy agenda *has to have risks*. There is no alternative.

I remember speaking to my client Charles about his high-flying job in finance that he loathed. He was dispirited and exhausted. His real passion was to get into corporate marketing. The trouble was that he wanted assurances and guarantees before he did anything about this. He was adamant that he wanted the transition to happen seamlessly; he wasn't prepared to jeopardise his sumptuous lifestyle, even for a few months. Even though Charles was a single young man of twenty-seven with no dependants he was still terrified of taking any sort of risk. He wanted a meaningful life but he wasn't prepared to take the steps to have it.

Sadly, Charles is still plodding along unhappily in his job. I hope that at some point in his life he will realise that it's worth taking a risk to find happiness.

Compare this attitude with the calibre of a Sally Becker, a Roger Bannister, an Emily Pankhurst, a George Stratford or even my own brother Brian, who I talked about in Chapter seven. Remember that Brian left a sumptuous lifestyle to return to Ireland with seven dependants and no guarantee of paid employment whatsoever. This was a monumental gamble. If any of these individuals had waited for a safe, guaranteed time to take action they would never have made their move; they'd still be in the starting position. As it was, each of them pulled the trigger on their own starting pistol. They didn't wait for anyone or anything else before going after what they truly wanted.

ARE YOU READY TO PULL THE TRIGGER?

Staying in your comfort zone means no stretching, no changing, no risking a journey into uncharted waters. But this only works for as long as it takes you to wake up to what you're really missing – the excitement and rush of cutting loose, and admitting what would really, really stretch and delight you. The degree of risk you take determines the degree of excitement you feel. I don't mean ridiculous risks like driving up the motorway the wrong way. I mean risks that matter, that bring you closer to what you really want.

EXERCISE

Ask yourself about your comfort zone. What are you comfortable with and what is outside that zone. How would you know that you were outside it? What two things that you would really, really like to have, do or be, would create uncertainty and discomfort for you?

Now asterisk the strongest one, the one that creates the most uncertainty, that would take you furthest out of your comfort zone. That's the one you're going to work on in this chapter!

Write it down and keep it because we'll come back to it later.

Life rewards Action. To take action towards your biggest desire is one of the most exhilarating things you can do for yourself. Even thinking about it should give you an endorphin rush! If not then you're still operating within the safety of your comfort zone, your security blanket, and you need to re-think your goal. Perhaps you've mastered one area of your life to the detriment of another? Are you a high achiever at work, with no time for a romantic life? Immersing yourself in work so that there are few opportunities to develop a relationship can be a sure way of avoiding the one thing that would perhaps test and terrify you. Look closely at your life and find the area in which you've played things really safe. Then look for the challenge you want to master.

EXERCISE

Think about the everyday decisions you make that contain and box you in. Are there fashions you long to wear but wouldn't dare? Are there shops, hotels or restaurants that you have decided are too grand for you or where you'd feel out of place? If so then make the decision to confront the boundary you've set yourself and push against it.

Over the next few days take yourself into one of these forbidden places. Browse in a stylish shop or have tea in a fabulous hotel. However daunted you feel, just take yourself right along there, hold your head up, smile and expect to be liked, and enjoy yourself.

It's the same with people. Are there people who you like and admire but dare not risk getting to know? Make a list of them and give each a rating from 1 to 10, based on how far out of your comfort zone they appear. Choose one person from this list to work on. Push through the boundary by arranging to meet them or stopping for a chat when previously you would have avoided them.

MY BULLET-PROOF SURVIVAL GUIDE FOR LIFE OUTSIDE THE COMFORT ZONE

I remember coaching Richard to get comfortable with the idea of moving to a new job that we'd been working together to achieve for some months. It was a massive leap upwards in terms of responsibility and pay and as his starting date drew closer he grew increasingly anxious. We both knew that he was a long way out of his comfort zone. I reminded Richard that it was perfectly natural for him to feel this way. Months ago we had planned that he would live a bit more dangerously and simply handle the consequences as they came along. Now the time had come.

This is the six-step bullet-proof plan that I gave him for handling his challenge and one that you can use for yourself for life outside your comfort zone.

STEP ONE — ENJOY THE FEELING

Fear can be exhilarating and give you a rush of energy and excitement. Many people interpret this as a bad thing – a sensation to be avoided. Not necessarily so. The hormones that fear and excitement produce are the same. When they course through your bloodstream, only you decide whether it's a surge of fear or excitement that you're experiencing.

I believe that many people live such safe lives and are so firmly entrenched in their comfort zones that they rarely experience intense enthusiasm or excitement. And when they do, they interpret these emotions as fear and as a sign that something is wrong. It isn't. Living with enthusiasm, optimism and passion is one way of knowing that you're fully alive and living right out on the edge of your potential. And if you've come this far with me it's because that's what you want for yourself, to live your best life, to be the best you can be, to live fearlessly.

Living your best life means that you will be moving out of your comfort zone on a regular basis. There is no avoiding this if you are to stretch yourself, to challenge yourself to live out your deepest desires and to refine yourself to be the best you can possibly be. So refuse to let fear paralyse you and instead turn it into excitement and let it propel you forward, out of your comfort zone.

Use this bullet-proof guide as your parachute. Use every tool, tip and technique that you've read in this book or any other. Pull out all the stops to make moving out of your comfort zone exciting, challenging and interesting.

Of course, there may be discomfort. As you discard your warm, familiar security cloak you will definitely notice the difference. But where others would scuttle back inside again I want you to brave the outside world, with all your support and know-how in place, so that you can enjoy yourself as you do it.

Get used to feeling comfortable with a little discomfort and a little uncertainty alongside a great deal of positive expectancy. Turn anxiety into anticipation, fear into energy and worry into action.

When Richard realised he was out of his comfort zone, we

simply activated this survival guide, starting with this first step of enjoying the feeling and viewing it as excitement. Even his physical reactions, such as nausea, could be seen as part of that excitement and anticipation.

Actors and musicians wouldn't be fired up enough to give great performances if they didn't experience the boost of fear and excitement-fuelled adrenaline beforehand.

Eleanor Roosevelt, wife of the US President, said: 'You gain strength, courage and confidence by every experience in which you really stop to look fear in the face. You are able to say to yourself, "I lived through this horror. I can take the next thing that comes along" . . . You must do the thing you cannot do.'

STEP TWO – TOUGHEN UP

Earlier in the book I asked you consciously to take charge of your mental programming by exerting more control over your thoughts and spoken words. This is the time to reinforce that new habit, because the time when you most need this approach is when the going gets tough. And that may be the time when you are least likely to remember it! When you're facing a major challenge, tap into the reserves of brilliance, strength and ingenuity that you have waiting. Don't buckle under the weight or let yourself down. Stand tall in your resolve and back yourself. The actions and decisions you take at a time of crisis have the potential to forge a new, stronger identity for yourself. The Chinese symbol for 'crisis' is composed of two characters: one representing danger and the other opportunity. Your opportunity at a difficult or challenging time is to stand up for yourself, to believe in yourself and to come through shining. So at a critical time you must watch, even more than at any other time, what you are saying and thinking about yourself. Remember the words of Henry Ford: 'Whether you think you can or you can't, you're right!'

Here are some of the affirmations I give to clients outside their comfort zones:

- *I like myself (say this one a lot).*
- *The more I relax and let go the more I get done.*
- *I trust myself completely.*
- *I approve of myself totally.*

Remember that you condition your emotional state with your thoughts and words and avoid torturing yourself. When a client is panicking my question is always: 'What have you been saying to yourself?' The answers are always, without exception, terrifying! Anyone would feel fear and panic with those thoughts swimming around in their head. Don't do this to yourself. You can only be panic-stricken if you think panic-inducing thoughts. Exercise self-discipline and pull back. Don't draw to yourself what you don't want.

STEP THREE – RELAX

When your mind is calm you are capable of so much more. One way of switching off and resting your mind is to tackle anxiety by physically relaxing your body. Exercise is a brilliant way to do this. I personally love running, but you may prefer exercise classes, taking a long walk or a round of golf. Others swear by squash or tennis. Yoga is a wonderful way of generating internal composure, as are the 'soft' martial arts such as T'ai Chi. I also strongly recommend that you begin the habit of meditation. Transcendental meditation is the simplest form to learn and there are lots of courses available if you want to take one.

Otherwise try this: Put aside as little as ten minutes every day to have some quiet time to yourself. Create the right atmosphere by lighting candles, burning oils or incense and playing ambient music. Sit upright so that you don't fall asleep. Then all you have to do is to allow your thoughts to pass by, without holding on to them. Obviously the more you do this the easier it becomes and the quicker you will drop into a deep state of relaxation.

Regular meditation like this has been scientifically proven to reduce your need for sleep. Twenty minutes of conscious relaxation is the equivalent of two hours' sleep.

The busier and more demanding your external world the more you need to cultivate stillness and steadiness in your internal world. You must withdraw from the hurly burly to recharge your batteries and refresh your mind. Physical relaxation and mental clarity go hand in hand. When everyone else is running around in a panic you will be the one who is thinking clearly and seeing the way forward. With clarity and internal composure you will have the best perspective.

Both men and women can be drama queens, frittering vast amounts of time and energy flapping and indulging in the rigmarole going on. You don't do this; you are a rock. You move with a steady gaze, a sharp focus and a clear head. You have calmed the internal chatter that most people live with. You are serene and poised and you have unshakeable internal composure. Very little rattles you and when it does you handle it quietly, on your own, with dignity. When most people run round in circles, vastly overreacting, you remain constant. Remember that powerful people talk less and think more.

STEP FOUR – DON'T TAKE YOURSELF TOO SERIOUSLY
Learn to laugh. Laughter is one of the most effective and under-estimated stress-relievers. Even putting a smile on your face,

regardless of how you actually feel will convey feelings of lightness and happiness to the rest of your body. The simple act of turning your mouth up at the corners cools the blood flow to the brain, which, researchers have found, makes you more relaxed. Put a smile on your face at all times, especially the worst ones. Laugh at yourself. Take yourself out with the lightest, most loyal friend you have and laugh at yourself, in the nicest way. Go to a comedy club or rent a brilliant comedy video.

Laughter therapy can even be used to help cure serious illness. In his book *Anatomy of an Illness*, former US magazine editor Norman Cousins describes how he cured himself of rheumatoid arthritis of the spine with laughter. Cousins discharged himself from hospital when his body was wracked with pain. He headed straight to his local video store and hired all the Marx Brothers films they stocked. He watched hour after hour of side-splitting comedy and saw that he could generate his own pain relief from laughter.

Patch Adams, whose story was made into a film starring Robin Williams, was a natural comedian who discovered the power of laughter over illness when he became a medical student. He used to go along to the children's wards in the hospital where he trained, dressed as a clown, and make them laugh. Although the authorities disapproved, many of Patch's patients improved immensely on his laughter medicine. When Patch qualified as a doctor he opened his own institute where laughter became as vital to health as the medical treatment.

Just think what you can do for your own spirit with laughter.

STEP FIVE – KNOW THAT YOU WILL SURVIVE
Give yourself breathing space to remember: 'This too will pass.' Claire Rayner, novelist and agony aunt says: 'I was taught the phrase "this too will pass" by my grandmother, to be used at *all*

times in your life. When things are spectacularly dreadful; when things are absolutely appalling; when everything is superb and wonderful and marvellous and happy, say these four words to yourself. They will give you a sense of perspective and help you also to make the most of what is good and be stoical about what is bad.'

However bad you feel, whatever the physical symptoms of your discomfort, please remember that *you will survive*. You will also recover more quickly than you expect. As human beings we handle things far better than we imagine we will. We cope, we pull through, we find the extra resources and we endure. Whether your upset lasts ten minutes or ten days, you will handle it. Life only demands from you the strength you possess. You are far, far stronger than you think.

STEP SIX – TALK TO GOD

Everyone needs something to hold on to. It's good to believe in something. Open up to the idea that there is a benevolent God, cosmic spirit or universal power available to you for support. It's pretty desperate to feel that you are alone in life with no greater force to turn to. I don't recommend going through life without this higher spiritual assistance, comfort and counsel. In my difficult moments I always turn my dilemma over to God and I always feel the response in the shape of additional insights and strength. I have even experienced remarkable 'coincidences' where practical assistance has come my way just when I really needed it.

Make a practice of writing down your requests for help before you sleep and on waking. Then write the answers and the solutions. I have never been lost for the right words when I have done this. Take a look at the best-selling book *Conversations with God* by Neale Donald Walsch. In this book he chronicles his questions to God and the answers he felt God was offering him. He kept a written record of the answers and that record became a series of books that became best-sellers around the world.

I have already mentioned in the chapter on beliefs the proven power of prayer. Not only can it improve the health of those we pray for – whether they know we are praying for them or not – but it can improve our own health and wellbeing.

John Maltby, a senior psychologist at Sheffield Hallam University, studied the effect of religion on the wellbeing of 500 students. 'We found that personal prayer was the most important factor, rather than simply being religious or attending services. The students who prayed suffered less from anxiety and depression.'

Whether these findings indicate the presence of a divine energy depends on your interpretation. Dr Maltby says: 'We think that it is the process of praying and taking time out from the hassles of life that brings the benefits – not the presence of God.'

The message seems to be that conventional religion is not a requirement; positive effects can derive from having something to believe in. Turning the problem over to this greater force in the 'Thy Will be Done' spirit, allows us to let go of the pressure and tension we place on ourselves.

EXERCISE

Earlier you highlighted the thing you wanted to have, do or be that took you furthest out of your comfort zone. Bring it to the table now and take a good look at it. Make the decision this instant to get comfortable with it. The way you do this is to draw up a plan of action to move you in the direction of this forbidden desire, whether it's a change of job, a new relationship, running a marathon or making your peace with a close friend or relative.

Take action today, begin right now to blow apart the four walls of your confinement. Feel those walls heave and slide further and further apart as you get bigger and bigger, taking up more space for yourself. Use the bullet-proof guide and enjoy the glorious feeling of pride and self-respect that only comes to people like you, who live and act fearlessly.

Heroes and heroines are brave not because they don't feel fear but because they act in spite of their fear. This is who you must be. Breathe a little bit deeper. Be a little bit more outstanding.

SURVIVAL OF THE TOUGHEST

Some people are thrown into circumstances so daunting and fearful that they could easily be forgiven for giving up. Yet these are often the people who display the most courage, the toughest spirit and the kind of dogged determination that makes them enormous successes despite the horrors with which they have had to cope. Chris Moon is one such person.

CHRIS'S STORY

CHRIS HAS RUN MORE THAN TWENTY MARATHONS, DESPITE HAVING LOST AN ARM AND A LEG IN A LAND MINE ACCIDENT. HIS AMAZING DETERMINATION HAS BEEN TOPPED ONLY BY HIS BRAVERY IN THE FACE OF DEATH. CHRIS WAS CLEARING ANTI-PERSONNEL MINES IN MOZAMBIQUE IN 1994 WHEN HE WAS BLOWN UP BY A MINE AS HE WAS WALKING IN A SUPPOSEDLY MINE-FREE AREA. 'I HAD THE MOST TERRIBLE FEELING OF DOOM AND I KNEW I SHOULDN'T STAY WHERE I WAS,' HE SAYS. 'I WALKED THREE PACES WHEN A MINE BURIED DEEP BELOW THE SURFACE, BEYOND METAL DETECTOR RANGE, EXPLODED.'

CHRIS LAY CRITICALLY WOUNDED, BUT STILL CONSCIOUS. HE SAW THAT HIS RIGHT HAND WAS MANGLED AND HIS RIGHT LOWER LEG HAD COMPLETELY GONE. DESPITE BEING IN AGONY AND NEAR DEATH HE REFUSED TO GIVE IN TO ANY NEGATIVE EMOTIONS.

'The easiest instinct was to die, but I knew I had to rise above it. I remember thinking "I don't deserve this" but nor would I allow myself to feel self-pity.'

His right arm was amputated to just below the elbow and his right leg to just below the knee. Chris had morphine immediately after the operation but then refused all further painkillers. 'I felt it was important to come to terms with the pain,' he explains. Chris chose to rely on no one but himself. 'I saw my recovery and future life as a huge issue of dignity and self-respect. I decided to use what happened to me as an opportunity to do something different.'

Within a year of his accident Chris got a Master's degree. He then started his own human resources and security management consultancy firm, called Making the Best. He became involved with many charities for the disabled and is an ambassador for the Prince's Trust, the Prince of Wales' charity foundation. Chris also married and had a son, and he began running marathons, including the Trans Sahara 240km (143-mile) race, known as the toughest race on earth. 'I like to see how far I can go,' he says. 'And for me failure is simply not an option. Whenever I've had to dig deep into my inner resources I've never felt there wasn't anything there.'

Richard's story

Richard Moore has also turned a traumatic experience into an opportunity to do great things. In 1972, Richard was ten and growing up amidst the troubles of Northern Ireland when he was shot and blinded by a soldier. 'I have no bitterness towards the man who shot me,' Richard says. 'I would like to meet him to show him that, even though I lost my eyesight, I have made something positive out of the

DREADFUL THING THAT HAPPENED TO BOTH OF US THAT DAY. I
REALISED I HAD A BIGGER PART TO PLAY IN THE WORLD. I HAD BEEN
A VICTIM OF WARFARE BUT HAD MANAGED TO GET MY LIFE
TOGETHER AND COULD HELP OTHERS DO THE SAME.'

RICHARD WENT ON TO SET UP THE CHARITY CHILDREN IN
CROSSFIRE, BRINGING CHILDREN AND ADULTS IN TROUBLED SPOTS
ALL OVER THE WORLD TOGETHER, ON A CROSS-COMMUNITY, CROSS-
BORDER BASIS AND MAKING A DIFFERENCE TO THE LIVES OF
THOUSANDS.

THE POWER OF PERSEVERANCE

For others, too, the notion of failure is simply not an option. Many
have achieved great success in the face of huge odds by refusing to
be daunted or to give up and heading steadily towards their goals.
Fred Smith, the founder of Federal Express, is one of them. He
came up with the idea for a company that would deliver overnight
packages around the world when he was at one of America's top
business schools. His teachers, some of the best business minds in
the States, gave him a C-minus for his paper, telling him that the
idea was ridiculous as people already used the mail service.

Undaunted, Fred put all his money into setting up his service.
On the first day he hoped to send 167 parcels. He actually sent two.
But Fred refused to see this as failure. He knew that if he could send
two parcels successfully all he needed to do was to increase the
numbers. Today FedEx is a billion-dollar organisation and Fred's
personal income is $50 million a year.

James Dyson, inventor of the massively successful Dyson vacuum
cleaner, gave up his job and almost went broke spending two years
making dozens of unsuccessful models. His final product revo-
lutionised the concept of vacuum cleaning, became Britain's most
popular model and made him a rich man.

Writer Joanna Rowling, author of the Harry Potter books, also persevered against the odds. She wrote her first book when she was a penniless single parent with a small daughter, living on benefits. She wrote her book by hand, sitting day after day over a coffee in a café while her daughter slept in her pushchair next to her. When she finally finished her book, after many months, she sent it off to an agent who rejected it as being far too long for children. Joanna's reaction was not to change her book, she simply sent it off to another agent, who loved it.

Her book became a publishing phenomenon, loved by children around the world and it changed the concept of what a children's book could be. The film rights were sold to Hollywood for £1 million and she went on to write three more Harry Potter books in a series that is planned to extend to seven. Her first three books sold 19 million copies in the States alone. This year Joanna is expected to make £80 million from her creation, making her one of Britain's richest women. And in a recent poll she was voted Britain's second favourite author of all time, more popular than Shakespeare and second only to Roald Dahl.

FAILURE IS NOT AN OPTION
Failure was never an option for Chris Moon, Richard Moore, Fred Smith, James Dyson or Joanna Rowling. From this day forth I insist that it be the same for you. The fear of failure has the potential to prevent you from taking the first step towards the thing that would make your life more meaningful, fun and fulfilling. So you have to handle your fear of failure and be willing to overcome it. I have gone through this issue with many, many clients and as a result I have learned exactly what is necessary in order to get the upper hand on this one. Here is my definitive 'Failure is not an option' plan.

FAILURE IS A FALLACY

The real truth is that once you take action there is no such thing as failure. There are only experiences, decisions and their consequences, and results. The only real failure is not having a go in the first place. If anything is worth doing it's worth doing poorly at first. In other words, stop being so hard on yourself and forget about trying to be perfect from the outset. Build failure into your plan so that you're not hung up on getting it right straightaway.

LEARN FROM YOUR MISTAKES

Learn and learn quickly. Not everyone learns from their mistakes. Most people are so busy feeling bad about themselves and giving themselves a hard time that they fail to see the treasure trove of information waiting to be claimed. Henry Ford went broke three times before he invented the car. He said: 'Failure is merely an opportunity to more intelligently begin again.' Adopt 'inverse paranoia' and believe that everything and everyone is conspiring to provide you with valuable lessons and opportunities. The most important thing is to learn from experience. You will eventually triumph when you know what you want and move towards it in a strategic, consistent, meaningful and purposeful manner. Just keep taking action and you'll keep getting results, and eventually they will be the results you want.

PUT ALL THOUGHTS OF FAILURE OUT OF YOUR MIND

Turn yourself into someone who is totally solution-oriented. As soon as setbacks present themselves, your natural unstoppability will kick in. See every problem as a gift. Look for the solution. Further, look for the benefit. How can you develop yourself by tackling the issue and ultimately triumphing? How can you improve on the original plan, from this extra information? What will you do differently and better as a result of what you now know? There's nothing wrong with fearful thoughts as long as you temper them with courageous and self-reliant thoughts.

With hindsight you may well come to be thankful for a setback that required you radically to re-think or to change course altogether. Bill Wyman was a member of one of the most successful rock bands in the world, but he may never have joined the Rolling Stones if his father had let him stay at school. 'School was going well,' he says. 'I was fifteen and about to take my O levels when one day my father said; "Right, I've had enough of you in that school, you're leaving." I did think he's stopped my chance of being educated, he'd knocked the next rung of the ladder out. But eventually I got into music and it didn't matter any more.' The rest, as they say, is history.

DON'T TAKE IT PERSONALLY
The real problem with failure and perceived failure is that people take it personally. It triggers and adds to underlying doubts and fears that they already harbour about themselves and confirms their beliefs about not being good enough or capable enough. Avoid this at all costs by simply recognising it. Being turned down, rejected or refused does not mean that you are incapable, wrong or bad. It simply gives you information, that you need to try again in a different way.

Don't dwell on failure or rejection, simply move on to find the solution that's waiting for you along the line. When it comes to taking action in the face of fear remind yourself that you've done it before, many times. You took a chance when you went from crawling to walking, when you swam for the first time, when you learned to ride a bike, when you moved away from home, when you asked for that date, when you changed jobs or moved towns.

In each of these situations you left behind the familiar to reach for something more. That reaching broadens your horizons and allows you to develop your own competence and worldliness.

KNOW YOU CAN HANDLE IT

Train yourself to be someone who just *knows* you can handle it. This is ultimately the most liberating truth that will underpin your whole life. Whether it's taking a risk with a relationship, leaving a well-paid job to do what really excites you or starting up something new, just know that, whatever happens, *you can handle it*. The future belongs to the risk-takers, not the security-seekers. Life is perverse in that the more you seek security, the less of it you have. That's because one of the fundamental lessons in life is that true security comes from inside us, not from outside. So the more you step out and seek opportunity, the more likely it is that you will achieve the security you desire.

STOP WORRYING

What you dwell on grows . . . so be careful. Worry is not just an awful waste of time and precious energy; it's far more dangerous than that. Worry is negative goal-setting. When you worry you are dwelling on, talking about and vividly imagining exactly what you don't want. If you worry long and hard enough about something, you are going to attract it into your life. My antidote to worry is twofold. First of all look at the worst that could possibly happen. Then laugh in the face of your ultimate fear and it will weaken and crumble. Your worst fears only have power over you when you refuse to face and feel them. Whatever you resist, persists.

People spend enormous amounts of time, effort and money suppressing their fears through over-eating, over-drinking, smoking, hours of television and taking drugs, both recreational and prescribed. In reality it would be so much easier to just hold up the fear, look it in the eye and laugh. You can try this with physical pain, whether it's toothache or childbirth! Confront the pain head-on, focus all your attention on it, breathe into it and watch it subside.

Remind yourself that if your worst fears actually did happen, guess what? *You'd handle it.*

The second part of my antidote to worry is to commit to doing everything in your power to ensure that this outcome does not actually happen. In other words, take action, and massive amounts of it. Conquer your worries by focusing exclusively on your mission and crank up your to-do list. Double the number of calls you make, get up earlier, give yourself far more to do than you previously thought reasonable. Get some results on the table. And, since the conscious mind can only hold one thought at a time, make sure it's a productive one.

BE PERSISTENT

It takes courage to endure, to persist, to stay at it once you have begun. Persistence is a form of courage, and one of the rarest forms. When you plan your work and work your plan through with persistence, even in the face of disappointment and unexpected setbacks, you will build and develop the quality of courage within you.

The vast majority of 'overnight successes' are nothing of the sort. They are the result of years of hard slog, ups and downs and dark nights of uncertainty. Even examples of terrific good luck are rarely that.

Take the story of one man's absolute determination to appear on the hit television show *Who Wants to be a Millionaire.* Paddy Spooner had already won £100,000 on the Australian version of the show and on his return to England he decided to try his luck on the British show. Unbelievably he succeeded and won another £250,000. The programme makers described the chances of appearing twice as 'incalculable'. But from the moment he won his first cheque Paddy had decided he would have another go back home. He was undeterred by reports that it was virtually impossible to get through on the phone lines, the first step to becoming a contestant. 'I reckoned it was a gamble worth taking,' he said. 'In the end it only took 400 attempts.' Before he appeared on the first show Paddy was broke and sleeping on a friend's floor. Now he's travelling around the world on his winnings.

Look at some other examples of dogged persistence: Thomas Edison was once asked how he managed to persist in his search to invent the light bulb. He answered: 'I have found 500 ways that didn't work . . . I am not discouraged, because every wrong attempt discarded is another step forward.'

The French Lieutenant's Woman, now considered a literary classic, was turned down by fifty publishers before author John Fowles found one who agreed to take it.

Nelson Mandela spent thirty years in prison as a result of his fight for the rights of black South Africans. For many of them he was kept in appalling conditions and was told that he had no hope of release. Yet he kept his courage, wisdom and optimism. When he was finally released he walked out of the prison with the utmost dignity and went on to become the President of South Africa – and a loved and revered figure worldwide.

JUST DO IT!

If you want to succeed, just take the next step and the one after that and keep going. If you're still hesitating it's because you're caught up in one or both of the two deadly habits of *procrastination* and *perfectionism*. Let me explain how they operate.

PROCRASTINATION

We put off what we fear. This is the essence of procrastination. We fear that our shortcomings will be revealed, so we avoid the moment of truth and the pain it will surely bring. Whether it's making that important call, asking for a pay rise or going on an exciting date, what we fear most is rejection.

The only antidote to this deadly thief of time is to *do it now*. Do the thing you fear most. Put that difficult call right at the top of your list; don't waste time thinking about it, just do it.

PERFECTIONISM

Wanting to get things perfect is the outcome of feeling 'not good enough' and needing other people's approval. But trying to be perfect gets you caught up in a spiral of exhausting and relentless struggle and competition. The craving to look good in front of other people becomes your driving force.

Refuse to go down this path. Admire yourself for what you are and forget about trying to prove that you're a superior human being. And remember to build in celebration and acknowledgment along the way, in order to fuel the next stage of your journey. Without this you'll dry up and burn out. Success breeds success . . . but only if you notice your successes in the first place. So take the time to congratulate yourself regularly.

Right now note down twenty achievements in your life that you're proud of. Build the habit of paying attention to your progress daily. Soak in a hot bath and luxuriate in your efforts.

YOUR ASSIGNMENT

Your assignment is to live with more verve, more courage and heroism than ever before. Keep in mind the glorious examples of the individuals in this chapter. If they could make of their lives what they have, then you can take risks and bring more zeal and daring into your life. Commit from this day onward to taking more risks, daring to be outstanding and being your absolute best, and grow into the kind of person whose internal strength and sheer guts defines you.

You have no limits because you know that absolutely anything is possible.

AND REMEMBER . . .

Failure is an indispensable part of success.

Every failure makes you stronger.

Your fear of failure is the greatest obstacle.

Fear can produce energy and excitement.

To reach your goals you must leave your comfort zone.

Life outside the comfort zone is a life worth living.

No setback is big enough to stop you.

There is nothing in life that you can't handle.

EPILOGUE

A Life Less Ordinary

Congratulations!

Well Done for staying the course. You've come a long way and kept with me this far. I want you to stay on track from here on. There's absolutely no turning back now. You have initiated a journey and a momentum that compels you to keep on keeping on with the challenge of moving your life in the direction of your deepest desires and heartfelt wishes.

You began your journey when you picked up this book, and if you've come this far then you're undoubtedly one of the brave few who is willing to live fearlessly, to face life head on, with courage and grit. You bring passion, enthusiasm and spirit to the table.

You are not naïve. You know that stepping out, going for what you want, involves taking risks and chances, encountering setbacks and obstacles and facing and handling disappointments, because *that's who you are*. You are big enough to face rejection and your fear of failure because you don't take any of it personally. You understand that mistakes are part of the dues one pays for a full life. You know that if you don't risk anything, you risk even more. And this knowledge frees you to be more daring, to step out and tread where others only gaze and fear. You know that while you may be disappointed if you fail, you are doomed if you don't try. This is the price to be paid for living *a bigger life*.

Facing possible disappointment is a small price to pay for a life less slow, less lumpen and less ordinary – for a life more shiny. Don't ever stop trying. The glory is not in never failing, but in getting back up and carrying on every time you fall. Energy creates energy. It is by spending yourself that you will become rich. Spend yourself well, but above all, *spend yourself.* Don't save yourself for another day. Take your chances while you have them. Life is precious, but don't be precious in the way you live it. Don't tiptoe around it. Honour it, and yourself, by giving it everything you've got, and more. Acknowledge your fears, but don't let them govern you. Move way beyond them. And one day you'll turn around and notice who you've become and smile.

Go for it. Live your life fearlessly. Be the hero of your own story.

GO FOR IT!

I have set up a Lifecoach line to keep you on track and to maintain your momentum and confidence. A team of qualified Coaches will support you in taking time to look at the direction of your life and to make the changes you really want. Get inspired to make your shifts and changes and make them stick by hiring your own coach.

You can also have occasional consultations to keep you boosted. This will pay dividends by supporting you in getting the results you want from life.

Simply call Lifecoach Line on 0906 636 1188.

STAY IN TOUCH

Write to me and let me know how you get on! I'd be delighted to get your progress reports and I'll keep you informed of my seminars and new books and tapes.

Email me at: fiona@lifecoachline.com

Or write to me at: Fiona Harrold, PO Box 4248, Goring-on-Thames, Oxfordshire, RG8 9XL, UK

You can also get information on lifecoaching seminars and training by contacting the Lifecoaching Academy (U.K.) on 0800 783 4823.